Supply Chain Planning and Analytics

Supply Chain Planning and Analytics

The Right Product in the Right Place at the Right Time

Gerald Feigin, PhD

Supply Chain Planning and Analytics: The Right Product in the Right Place at the Right Time
Copyright © Business Expert Press, LLC, 2012.

First published in 2011 by
Business Expert Press, LLC
222 East 46th Street, New York, NY 10017
www.businessexpertpress.com

ISBN-13: 978-1-60649-245-1 (paperback)

ISBN-13: 978-1-60649-246-8 (e-book)

DOI 10.4128/ 9781606492468

A publication in the Business Expert Press Supply and Operations Management collection

Collection ISSN: 2156-8189
Collection ISSN: 2156-8200

Cover design by Jonathan Pennell
Interior design by Scribe Inc.

First edition: August 2011

10 9 8 7 6 5 4 3 2 1

Printed in the United States of America.

For Juliette, Amanda, and Jennifer

Abstract

Supply chain planning is concerned with making decisions about how many goods to procure, make, and deliver before knowing exactly what the demand for products is going to be. These planning decisions are difficult because they must be made with uncertain and dynamic information about future demand, available production capacity, and sources of supply. This book focuses on the three interlinked processes that compose effective supply chain planning: demand planning, sales and operations planning, and inventory and supply planning. If executed well, these planning processes will help a company to achieve its targeted balance between efficiency and responsiveness. If executed poorly, they can be the root cause of any number of supply chain problems. This book describes these processes, how they are interconnected, and the practical challenges of implementing them. It also explains the important ways in which analytical tools and methods can be utilized to make better supply chain planning decisions.

Keywords

Supply chain planning, supply chain management, demand planning, forecasting, inventory planning, inventory management, supply planning, sales and operations planning, S&OP, business analytics, data analytics, supply chain analytics, production planning, distribution planning

Contents

Foreword

Whoever sets pen to paper writes of himself, whether knowingly or not.

—E. B. White

The writers of business books tend to fall into two camps: academics with PhDs and management consultants with MBAs. I do not fall neatly into either category. I have a PhD in applied mathematics but have worked in industry my entire career. I have done many things that professors typically do—taught courses to business school students, written technical papers in refereed journals, and authored patents. I have also been a full-time consultant for many years to businesses large and small, often collaborating closely with management consultants. In addition, I have worked for software companies and in the research division of IBM. In short, my career path has followed an irregular trajectory. That alone may not be enough to differentiate this book from others written on the same or similar subject. But it helps to explain the perspective that I bring to problems addressed in this book.

By training, I approach problems from an analytical, systems-oriented point of view. What this means in practice is that I tend to rely more on data and analysis when examining business problems than on the traditional management arts of experience and intuition. This approach is so ingrained that it took me some time to appreciate that others in the business world do not necessarily think about problems in the same way. This perspective, by the way, has gained currency in recent years under the catchphrase "business analytics." Though it is too early to say, it appears that this newfound interest in data-driven decision making may not be just a fad: Recent research suggests "that firms that adopt data-driven decision making have output and productivity that is 5–6% higher than what would be expected given their other investments and information technology usage."[1] For those of us who have been practicing this approach for years, this research is not surprising but provides much-needed confirmation of what we have suspected all along—namely, that an analytical approach to decision making really does lead to better outcomes.

When I completed graduate school in 1990, the work opportunities for PhDs in disciplines like applied mathematics and operations research were limited. Generally, one became a professor in the operations management department of a business school or in the industrial engineering or operations research department of a university. Or one went to work at an industrial research lab, like AT&T's Bell Labs or IBM's research division. I chose the latter.

My PhD was in applied probability, and I suppose if there is a common thread connecting my work as a PhD student to the topic of this book, it is my interest in decision making under uncertainty. I have always had a fascination with randomness and the various ways in which human beings attempt to cope with it. Planning is the bureaucratic term for decision making under uncertainty, and supply chain planning, at its core, is about preparing for uncertain future demand.

My approach to supply chain planning is informed by both my analytical way of thinking and my training in applied probability. I believe, for example, that future demand for a product can be characterized by a probability distribution, even if that distribution is unknown and is a function of many variables—some under a company's control, some not. At the same time, I am not in the mold of some academic thinkers, who all too often make convenient but inaccurate assumptions about the nature of randomness in the interest of mathematical elegance and analytical tractability. While I may appreciate the beauty of a mathematical model, I am much more interested in the practical application of that model than in its formal properties. I am happy to use whatever mathematical tools are at my disposal in the interest of solving a real business problem even if that solution is inelegant or imperfect.

I recognize that individuals for whom this book is written—business students and others who are interested in understanding the challenges of supply chain planning—have many competing claims on their time. With that in mind, I have deliberately kept this book short and to the point. I have kept many topics brief that could be greatly expanded on. The purpose of this book is to raise important practical issues in supply chain planning that have not received adequate attention in operations management textbooks. More often than not, the reason they have not received adequate attention is that they are thorny problems that do not have simple solutions. Having worked in the trenches all of my career wrestling with these problems, I know from firsthand experience that they are not trivial to solve. Yet my core belief is that analytical approaches can yield significant benefit in both framing the problems and finding solutions.

The power of computers at our disposal today together with the vast quantities of information that businesses now routinely collect is changing the way that businesses can tackle many kinds of problems. The use of analytical models to help solve supply chain planning problems will continue to grow as the data available become richer and computing horsepower to process that data continues to grow. My modest hope is that this book will aid in pointing to ways in which this kind of insight through data analysis and computer modeling can provide significant value.

Acknowledgments

I am grateful to the many people who graciously provided valuable feedback on the initial draft of this book and who engaged in helpful dialogue on various topics: Robert Baseman, Bala Chandran, Yves Dallery, Leon Hsu, Kaan Katircioglu, Tim Kniker, Ashok Mukherjee, Jim Schor, Robert Tevelson, Kermit Threatte, Loren Werner, and David Yao. I also want to thank Mitchell Burman and Jim Schor for encouraging me to write the book and for starting a company devoted to the idea of better decision making through analytics, long before it became fashionable. Finally, my deepest appreciation to everyone at Analytics Operations Engineering and to many individuals at the Boston Consulting Group and at IBM with whom I have had the pleasure to work over the years.

CHAPTER 1

Introduction

Supply chains cannot tolerate even 24 hours of disruption. So if you lose your place in the supply chain because of wild behavior you could lose a lot. It would be like pouring cement down one of your oil wells.

—Thomas Friedman

The array of products readily available to consumers today is astonishing. Yet most of us take for granted the supply chains that make and deliver these products. When we shop for goods, whether online or in stores, we expect to find products available. Although occasionally we need to wait longer than we'd like or have to accept another product as a substitute, we usually find what we are looking for. But if we are honest with ourselves, we know that it is a minor miracle that the product—any product—is sitting on the shelf when we seek it. To get the right product to the right place at the right time requires that a lot of things go right over the product's long journey from raw ingredients to final form. Opportunities for disruption arise at every step.

Supply chains fail in big and small ways. They can fail slowly over long periods because of systemic problems, such as those underlying the centralized planning economies of the Soviet Union and eastern bloc nations. Or they can fail suddenly and dramatically due to unexpected stresses, such as those caused by natural disasters. They also fail frequently in various smaller ways, as when products stock out in supermarkets because of demand spikes or when key industrial ingredients suddenly become scarce, such as drywall in the construction industry in 1999 or power transistors in the electronics industry in 2010.

While we may be aware of shortages or other supply chain problems that arise from time to time, the major challenges and inefficiencies of operating a supply chain are often hidden from view. But as anyone involved in supply chain operations knows, problems are plentiful. Malcolm Gladwell, in an article about the disposable diaper industry writes,

Out-of-stock rates are already a huge problem in the retail business. At any given time, only about ninety-two percent of the
products that a store is supposed to be carrying are actually on
the shelf—which, if you consider that the average supermarket
has thirty-five thousand items, works out to twenty-eight hundred
products that are simply not there. (For a highly efficient retailer
like Wal-Mart, in-stock rates might be as high as ninety-nine percent; for a struggling firm, they might be in the low eighties.)[1]

You can argue about whether an out-of-stock situation in a retail setting
causes greater harm to the retailer's sales or to the vendor whose product
has stocked out, but the harm to sales and profitability to both parties is
nonetheless real and significant.

The flip side of out-of-stock problems is excess inventory. Companies
invest a lot in inventory. According to the Bureau of Economic Analysis, U.S. domestic real manufacturing and trade inventories at the end of
first quarter 2010 amounted to approximately $1.3 trillion on annual-
ized sales of $11.5 trillion.[2] This means that for every $9 in annual sales,
approximately $1 is invested in inventory, of which roughly 25% is in
raw materials and work in progress (WIP) and 75% is in finished goods.
Most of this inventory, of course, is not excess, but companies in diverse
industries routinely write off 3% to 5% of inventory each year as excess
and obsolete, which translates to about $40 to $65 billion in inventory
every year that is thrown out, destroyed, or otherwise disposed of.

Even when supply chains seem to be functioning more or less properly, this does not mean they are being run at the right level of efficiency
and responsiveness. Efficiency is about cost effective use of assets; responsiveness is about providing the appropriate level of customer service, both
in terms of speed of response and in the assortment of products that are
available. Finding the right balance between efficiency and responsiveness
is a perennial challenge and one that is central to effective supply chain
management. An exclusive focus on efficiency leads to bizarre ends, as
Jagjit Singh recognized when he wrote about an efficiency expert who
visited a symphony concert at the Royal Festival Hall in London and
reported the following:

For considerable periods the four oboe players had nothing to do. The number should be reduced and the work spread evenly over the whole of the concert, thus eliminating peaks of activity. . . . Much effort was absorbed in the playing of demi-semi-quavers; this seems to be an unnecessary refinement. It is recommended that all notes should be rounded to the nearest semi-quaver.[3]

By the same token, an excessive focus on responsiveness leads to equally bizarre results, as Marshall Fisher explains in discussing the toothpaste industry:

A few years ago, I was to give a presentation to a food industry group. I decided that a good way to demonstrate the dysfunctional level of variety that exists in many grocery categories would be to buy one of each type of toothpaste made by a particular manufacturer and present the collection to my audience. When I went to my local supermarket to buy my samples, I found that 28 varieties were available. A few months later, when I mentioned this discovery to a senior vice president of a competing manufacturer, he acknowledged that his company also had 28 types of toothpaste— one to match each of the rival's offerings. Does the world need 28 kinds of toothpaste from each manufacturer?[4]

Undue attention to responsiveness can also be manifested in overly aggressive service-level targets. It's not unusual for companies to promise the same high level of service for all products and all customers. For example, one large computer manufacturer targets shipment of all orders within 10 days of order receipt, regardless of the type of computer ordered, the complexity of the order, the lead time for the parts, or the type of customer. Such a one-size-fits-all approach not only is expensive but also usually fails because companies don't make the necessary investment in inventory and resources to maintain such service levels across the board. Finding the right level of responsiveness requires making difficult choices about service-level differentiation: what level of service to provide to different customers and for different products. Adopting a uniform level of service across all products and customers may sound simple and egalitarian but almost never is the right choice.

Companies with inefficient or unresponsive supply chains can mask problems with extra inventory and through operational heroics, which amount to incurring extra costs to expedite orders that are in danger of being lost because of delays. Both of these fixes are expensive and the costs associated with them are often not easily visible, get built into the cost base over time, and are difficult to remove later. Nonetheless, they can be effective. As a result, companies often come to believe that these solutions—holding lots of inventory or having teams of expeditors—are a necessary cost of doing business. But often, they are necessary only because they are doing a poor job of supply chain planning.

About Supply Chain Planning and Analytics

To run a supply chain effectively requires smart supply chain planning. If your customers expect products to be available when they order them, you need to plan for adequate supply so that you can respond to orders as soon as they are placed. This is true regardless of the manufacturing or distribution philosophy that your company adopts: build-to-forecast, build-to-order, just-in-time, quick-response, mass-customization, sense-and-respond. All of these approaches require making decisions about what products to produce or procure before knowing what actual demand will result. For example, in the case of building products to order, you still need to anticipate and plan for enough supply in the form of parts and resources in order to effectively respond to orders when they arrive. The level at which planning needs to occur will change depending on the production model you follow, but supply chain planning remains a critical function in the operation of any supply chain.

In short, supply chain planning involves making decisions about what parts to procure and what products to produce before knowing what actual demand will result. These planning decisions are difficult because they must be made with uncertain and conflicting information about future demand, available production capacity, and sources of supply. In most companies, reaching these decisions is a highly complex balancing act, involving trade-offs along many dimensions (e.g., inventory targets versus customer service levels, older products versus newer ones, direct customers versus channel partners) and requiring the compromise of constituents—sales, marketing, operations, procurement, product development, finance, as well as suppliers and customers—with varied objectives and incentives. In short, the supply chain planning process is all about deciding the right level of responsiveness and efficiency to target and figuring out how to achieve these targets. The ability of a company to nimbly navigate this planning process without giving too much influence to any of the parties involved largely determines how well the company can respond to changing market conditions and ultimately whether the company will continue to thrive.

Uncertainty is at the heart of why supply chain planning is challenging and sometimes counterintuitive. A number of books have appeared in recent years that describe how easily human beings are fooled by randomness.[5] We see patterns where none exists, and we are susceptible to a variety of statistical biases that distort our understanding of the world. These distortions affect our ability to plan reliably. If you know that you are going to sell exactly 100 widgets and your supply is 100% reliable, matching supply with demand is fairly straightforward. But if you don't know the demand for widgets and your supply is unreliable or constrained, then the problem is not so simple. And yet this is exactly the situation many companies find themselves in.

Too often, supply chain planning is poorly defined and badly executed. Poor or ineffective supply chain planning processes can manifest themselves in a variety of ways. In many companies, operations personnel view themselves as the white knights whose role it is to meet the changing demands for products placed on them at any cost. This load-and-chase mentality may appeal to the can-do work ethic that many companies want to instill in their workers. But it is often symptomatic of a fundamental and unhealthy power imbalance between the sales organization and those responsible for product supply that leads frequently to inefficient and counterproductive decisions. For example, in one semiconductor manufacturing company, more than one-third of wafer lots in production at any given time are flagged as "hot," a designation that gives them priority over other jobs. The fact that so many lots are hot, though, coupled with the fact that the designations change day by day means that little is achieved in terms of reduced cycle times or better on-time delivery.

In other situations, we find exactly the opposite mentality: plant managers who are constantly second-guessing what the sales personnel are forecasting or making on-the-fly decisions on their own about what to produce because of insufficient guidance from the sales, marketing, and finance organizations. This situation sometimes arises when supply chain planning occurs at too high a level to be of practical value to the plant manager, who must frequently make decisions not only about what product lines to produce but also about what the volumes will be for the products that compose each product line. If the output of the planning process dictates that 10,000 Rapid Cool air conditioners are to be produced, the decision leaves much to the imagination of the plant manager, who has to decide on the basis of too little information how to allocate production of these 10,000 units among the 30 different models composing the Rapid Cool brand.

Even when the planning process does produce a production plan at the granularity needed by operations, the decision process is often flawed, resulting in poor product mix decisions that do not incorporate profit margin and market opportunity differences among different products. This type of problem arises from confusion between management objectives and forecasts. In a typical company, at least two different estimates of future demand are generated, both referred to as forecasts. One forecast—sometimes called a revenue forecast—is generated by starting with revenue projections made at the highest levels of a company and working down from there to a set of projections at a product family level that, when aggregated, will meet the revenue projections for the company. More often than not, these revenue projections are not estimates of the most likely revenue that the company will achieve; rather, they represent targets, sometimes highly aggressive, that the company would like to achieve. Another forecast, often called an unbiased forecast, is generated based on historical sales patterns and often use statistical methods—sometimes sophisticated but more often simple—to project the most likely estimates for future demand. These forecasts are usually generated at the most detailed level for which adequate sales data are available, often at a much lower level of granularity than the level at which the revenue forecast is generated.

The key observation frequently missed by companies is that these two forecasts, even when specified at the same level of granularity, are not estimates of the same quantity: The revenue forecast embodies an estimate of what the company's objectives are; the unbiased forecast reflects an estimate of the most likely demand to be realized. These two quantities are usually at odds, as they should be. Any participant in supply chain planning knows that the revenue forecast almost always exceeds the operations forecast. The discrepancy between these two forecasts is usually resolved by uniformly scaling the operations forecast upward so that, in aggregate, the operations forecast matches the revenue forecast. But in doing so, companies are missing a potentially enormous opportunity to improve profitability.

This book focuses on the three interlinked processes that compose supply chain planning: demand planning, sales and operations planning (S&OP), and inventory and supply planning. Some companies may refer to these planning activities by other names, but they all struggle with the ongoing effort of matching unknown future demand with sometimes variable and constrained supply. That is what these three processes are intended to accomplish. If executed well, these planning processes will help a company to achieve its targeted balance between efficiency and responsiveness. If executed poorly, they can be the root cause of any number of supply chain problems:

- Dissatisfied customers because products they order either are out of stock or arrive late
- Angry suppliers because purchase orders are constantly changing
- Excess procurement costs because of parts expediting
- Distribution headaches because expedited orders are blowing the logistics budget
- Production disruptions because parts are not available for half the production orders while the other half are being expedited
- Finance complaints because too much cash is tied up in working capital

Figure 1.1 describes the logical flow of the three processes composing supply chain planning. The process starts with demand planning, the objective of which is to create an unbiased forecast of future demand. The unbiased forecast is then utilized by S&OP to decide the right level of supply to target for products. The objective of the S&OP process is to utilize the unbiased forecast together with information about demand variability, supply availability, resource constraints, and revenue objectives to derive a

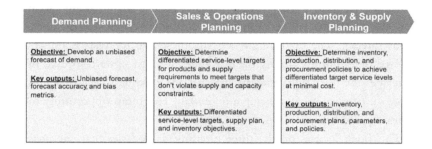

Figure 1.1. Three processes that compose supply chain planning.

set of service-level objectives for the company, as well as cost estimates to attain these objectives. The success of the S&OP process should be judged by how well the company meets these service-level and cost objectives. The last step in the process is inventory and supply planning, which is concerned with how to implement inventory, production, procurement, and distribution policies to achieve the sales and operations plan. The goal of inventory and supply planning is to determine exactly when parts or products need to be manufactured, ordered, and delivered to meet service-level requirements and cost objectives set by the S&OP process.

The objectives and interrelationships of these processes may appear simple and logical enough, but companies rarely get them right. Sometimes the problems are organizational in nature—for example, a lack of clarity on what groups in an organization have responsibility for which planning activities or a lack of end-to-end accountability for the results of the planning process. More frequently, however, the problems companies face have to do with the practical and technical challenges of executing each planning process effectively—that is, ensuring that the steps and outputs of each process are well defined and that the right software tools needed to carry out the processes are in place.

It is these practical challenges of supply chain planning on which this book is focused. My approach to addressing these challenges tends to be analytical. Thus this book is just as much about *supply chain analytics*—how analytical methods and data-driven decision making can be applied to improve supply chain planning—as it is about supply chain planning. Many operations management texts present mathematical methods and algorithms for solving certain classes of supply chain planning problems. This book is intended to complement these texts by focusing not only on the mathematical models but on the problems that arise in practice either that these models do not adequately address or that make applying the models difficult or impossible. The book is not intended to provide complete solutions to these problems but more to highlight the complexities and subtleties involved and describe ways to overcome practical issues that have worked for some companies. Where appropriate, I outline analytical approaches to solve problems that have not received adequate attention in existing textbooks. These descriptions are not rigorous algorithms and are only meant to suggest possible approaches. My hope is that they will be improved on and refined by others.

Supply Chain Planning Topics Addressed in This Book

The remainder of the book is divided into three chapters, one for each of the processes that compose supply chain planning. In the chapter on demand planning, the focus is on discussing common practical questions that frequently arise when deploying a demand planning process. The following are examples:

- What procedure should be utilized to remove promotion effects from past sales?
- What statistical methods are best at generating forecasts for what types of products?
- At what level of the product or geography hierarchy does it make most sense to forecast?
- Is it worthwhile to invest in a demand planning software system?
- What kind of improvement in forecast accuracy can you expect to obtain by investing in improving your forecasting processes?
- What are the right management metrics for demand planning, and how can these metrics be utilized to drive improvements in the demand planning process?
- What process should you use to forecast new products? End-of-life products?

Chapter 3, the chapter on S&OP, emphasizes the key role this process plays in shaping supply chain responsiveness—specifically, determining the service levels that the company should promise to different customers for different products given available supply, resource constraints, and uncertainty in demand. One of the basic levers that companies have to sell products is service-level differentiation. In many companies, this lever is rusty and stuck in place. A useful way to think of service-level targets is that they are a statement about how much of the unknown future demand for products a company wants to risk investment dollars preparing for. A 98% in-stock rate target for a product means you want to be prepared to satisfy 98% of unknown future demand from available in-stock inventory. Is this too high, too low, or just right? The answer depends on what it costs to stock to the 98th percentile of the demand distribution, whether you have the supply and capacity available to attain that supply level, the profitability of the product, and so on. This is precisely the decision that is central to S&OP. Examples of some of the practical challenges companies face in deploying an S&OP process that are discussed in chapter 3 include the following:

- How should you determine the appropriate level of service to target for different products and customers?
- How do you estimate demand variability and demand distributions? How should this information be incorporated into the S&OP process?
- How should revenue targets be incorporated into the S&OP process?
- How should supply and resource constraints be incorporated into the S&OP process?
- At what level of granularity should the S&OP process be performed?
- What software tools can be utilized to improve the S&OP process?

Chapter 4, the chapter on inventory and supply planning, focuses on the challenges of devising inventory, production, and distribution policies that achieve the sales and operations plan. Some of the questions discussed in this chapter are as follows:

- How do you disaggregate a sales and operations plan conducted at a product family level to the more detailed level needed for inventory and supply planning?
- If you use formulas to set safety stock targets to achieve a specified service level, how can you be sure that these formulas give correct results?
- How do you deal with lot-size restrictions, volume discounts, and joint-replenishment constraints when setting inventory replenishment policies?
- How should lead time variability be taken into consideration in determining safety stock requirements?
- What are the principal capabilities to look for in software systems that support inventory and supply planning?
- Are you storing inventory in forms and locations that make the most sense from both a customer serviceability perspective and an inventory perspective?

None of these questions has an easy answer; beware of anyone who claims otherwise. In some cases, my objective is simply to raise the questions and discuss pertinent aspects of them without having definitive answers. In others, I suggest possible analytical approaches to answering them.

The Elevator Pitch

Because much has been written about supply chain planning, a natural question arises about what is new in this book. For the benefit of the impatient reader, I highlight here certain key ideas that I believe have not received adequate attention elsewhere.

Demand Planning

- *Focus on forecast bias.* The metrics typically presented in operations management textbooks to evaluate the quality of a forecast are the mean absolute deviation (MAD), the mean squared error (MSE), and the mean absolute percentage error (MAPE). While there is a place for these metrics in forecast accuracy reporting within a company, I believe these metrics largely miss the point, which is that most often the biggest problems in forecasting arise because of systematic biases. Such biases will not be exposed by looking at these metrics. As a result, I believe the more important metric for companies to focus on is forecast bias, not forecast accuracy. In general, problems with systematic bias in forecasting are much easier to correct than poor forecast accuracy. If your forecast accuracy is poor, that may be due to inherent demand variability over which you may not have much control.

- *Autoselection.* Most books on forecasting and demand planning focus on statistical techniques for generating forecasts. But the question of how to select the best method to use in a particular instance has not received a lot of attention. One approach to tackling this problem is to automate it through an autoselection procedure. This is a dynamic procedure in which a computer system monitors the performance of a large number of statistical methods over time and, based on user-defined criteria, selects the best statistical method to use. Unfortunately, autoselection, sometimes referred to as "pick-best," does not have a good reputation because of erratic behavior that often occurs in poor software implementations. If implemented well, however, it is a powerful technique to overcome the difficult problem of selecting the best performing statistical method for a large number of stock-keeping units (SKUs).

Sales and Operations Planning

- *Service-level differentiation.* Unlike much of what has been written about S&OP, I argue that the key objective of S&OP is deciding what level of service to provide for different products and customers, taking into consideration demand variability, available supply, resource constraints, and working capital constraints and revenue objectives. Because a key part of the process is deciding how much risk to take in positioning supply against uncertain future demand, one of the central activities in S&OP is analyzing and characterizing demand variability and supply risks.

- *Revenue targets.* Some people view the S&OP process as simply a way to align the unbiased statistical forecast with the revenue targets for the company. In this view, all the S&OP process really accomplishes is to scale the forecast up to meet revenue targets. Such an approach is misguided and generally leads to poor results. There is a place for revenue targets in the S&OP process, but the S&OP process should have latitude to decide both the degree to which revenue targets should be taken into consideration and how scaling of the forecast should be carried out. Feedback mechanisms should be in place to ensure that the sales and operations plan does not simply reflect unconstrained sales aspirations.

Inventory and Supply Planning

- *Dynamic inventory control.* Much of the literature on inventory management focuses on the mathematics of how to set inventory parameters to achieve a given service-level target. But what if the formulas are incorrect? An important part of inventory planning is implementing a mechanism for automatically adjusting inventory levels in response to service levels being over- or underattained. I refer to this mechanism as dynamic inventory control or closed-loop inventory control. It is similar to the concept of control charts used in statistical process control and is a powerful way to manage inventory to achieve target service levels. Unfortunately, the technique is not widely used, largely because inventory management systems do not have this feature built in.
- *S&OP disconnect.* One of the frequent problems with supply chain planning is that different functions within an organization may perform planning activities that are not synchronized with other functions. One way in which this happens is if the S&OP process is performed at a product family or brand level and does not provide adequate guidance to inventory and supply planners to implement planning policies at an SKU level. If the sales and operations plan stipulates supplying 1,000 units of family X, how do planning personnel decide which

specific units in the family to supply? Their decision will be made without guidance from the S&OP process, and though their intentions may be good, they will be making a key decision without input from the key S&OP stakeholders. In order to avoid this disconnect, the S&OP process needs to provide differentiated service-level targets for different products and customers to the inventory and supply planning process. In turn, the inventory and supply planning process should be held accountable for achieving these targets.

These ideas and others are elaborated in the chapters that follow.

CHAPTER 2

Demand Planning

The only thing we know about the future is that it will be different.

—Peter Drucker

A question that is often asked in various guises in all kinds of businesses is, how much of this product are we going to sell? The answer is, it depends. It depends on who is asking the question, what product it is being asked about, what the state of the economy will be, what period of time you are looking at, how the product is priced relative to competition, whether there are substitutes available to customers, how the product has been or will be marketed, the product quality, where the product is available, and how quickly it can be provided to the customer.

Demand planning, or just plain forecasting, is what companies do when they attempt to answer this question. Many decisions within a company depend on its outcome: how much product is produced, how much inventory is stored, how much supply is procured, how much capacity is needed, what staffing is required, and what working capital is needed. And yet it is remarkable how little attention companies in general give to forecasting and how little thought goes into designing a process that will yield the best possible result. Usually relegated to a back-office operations staff or to a back-office software system, forecasting as a business process is not often treated with the seriousness it deserves.

Business forecasting has been around as long as businesses have. In the introduction to *The Problem of Business Forecasting*, written in 1924, William Foster wrote,

When a man enters business, he enters a forecasting profession. He may forecast badly or well, but forecast he must. He may scorn business forecasters, but he cannot help being one. He may shun statistics, but he cannot help using them. Since business is essentially risk-taking with the expectation of profits, every enterpriser must run risks; and, as a risk-taker, he is necessarily a business forecaster.[1]

In 1927, William Wallace published a book called *Business Forecasting and Its Practical Application*. He describes the critical need of forecasting in all businesses:

> We would sum up, therefore, by suggesting that every man or woman in business must forecast; and that such forecast must be based upon statistics (by whatever name they may be called). Every man who lives by selling goods, whether in a vast departmental store or in a village shop, if he is to be successful, must not only foresee the probable tastes of his customers, but must assess their probable purchasing power. This will depend upon their numbers and their income per head; and the latter in turn will depend upon the general state of trade. Every buyer of goods must not only know the quality and characteristics of the article he buys, but must make an estimate of the probable course of its prices. This, in turn, requires consideration of the probable supply of the article, the rate at which that supply will be increased or diminished as a result of a change in price, the demand for the article, and the extent to which that will be stimulated or checked by a reduction or increase in price respectively, the existing stocks, the possible substitutes, and the purchasing power of potential purchasers, leading again to the same ultimate inquiry into general trade prospects. Every manufacturer must estimate not only his position in relation to his competitors, but the probable price of his raw materials, the probable level of wages, the probable volume of his sales, the extent to which he must advertise, and so on. Until he does so, he cannot properly determine his price, his purchases, or his scale of production.[2]

In the years since Foster and Wallace wrote, a large number of books and articles have been published on the subject of forecasting, many of these focused on techniques for generating statistical forecasts.[3] The intent of this chapter is not to add to this already rich literature but rather to point out some of the remaining challenges in forecasting that companies continue to wrestle with and to suggest possible approaches to meeting these challenges.

While forecasting is an important process in every company, the idea that poor forecasting is the fundamental problem that prevents a company from succeeding—often expressed with the familiar refrain "if only we could get our forecast right, all of our problems will be solved"—is misguided. Just as misguided is the notion that if you only try hard enough, you can get a near-perfect forecast. At the same time, it's important to realize that forecasts can be made better and that it is often a worthwhile endeavor to do so. In fact, small improvements in forecasting can yield disproportionate supply chain cost savings. And that naturally leads to some key questions about forecasting: If you make an investment in forecast improvement, what is a reasonable expected return on that investment? Among all the initiatives that are competing for investment dollars within a company, is forecast improvement a worthwhile investment? And how should you make such an investment? In the later sections of this chapter, I provide some thoughts and guidelines for answering these difficult questions.

What Is a Forecast?

The end result of demand planning is a statement about future demand, which usually takes the form of a weekly or monthly estimate, by region or customer segment, of the quantity of a product that is to be sold over the next 6 to 12 months. It is often referred to as an *unconstrained* or *unbiased forecast* because it is not constrained by supply or other resources and ideally should not be biased upward or downward.

From a probabilistic viewpoint, a forecast is an estimate of the mean of an underlying demand distribution. Rarely in forecasting does any discussion arise about other relevant statistics about the demand distribution: the mode, the median, and higher moments of the distribution. By focusing almost exclusively on the mean demand, companies often lose sight of the critical importance of estimating demand variability. Rarely do companies attempt to estimate the shape of the demand distribution—for example, whether demand in a given period follows a normal distribution, a lognormal distribution, an exponential distribution, a beta distribution, or a triangular distribution. And yet the shape of the demand distribution—and in particular, the tail—yields a great deal of information about the nature of demand and has a significant impact on service levels and supply chains costs. Without good information about demand variability, companies are left to make critical decisions about what customer service levels to target and how to reasonably meet these targets on the basis of hunches or rules of thumb. In fact, one of the key activities of the sales and operations planning (S&OP) process is analyzing and characterizing demand variability so that this information can be incorporated into the decision about what customers service levels to target.

The creation of an unconstrained forecast is just the first step in the supply chain planning process. The unconstrained forecast is not a statement about what the company plans to produce or procure. To the casual observer, this may appear odd. After all, if you have an estimate of future demand, why would you not rely on this to decide what to produce and what to buy? The answer is that because the forecast is just a point estimate of the mean demand, you may not want to plan for meeting the mean demand but rather some quantity higher or lower than this. The decision about what the company should produce or procure requires taking into a consideration issues about demand uncertainty, supply constraints, production capacity, product profitability, and market share objectives. This decision is the outcome of the consensus-based S&OP process, a process that logically follows the initial demand planning process and that is taken up in chapter 3.

Generating an Unconstrained Forecast

Forecasting future demand for a product can seem like a hopelessly complex task since it depends on so many tacit assumptions. Where does one begin if so many assumptions need to be made and any one of them may be violated? Most companies proceed with the blanket assumption that the future will resemble the past—for example, pricing relative to competition will remain the same, the economy will continue on its recent trends, product quality will remain similar, and so on. With this assumption, it then becomes quite reasonable to base a forecast of future demand on recent past sales, which is by far the most common approach to forecasting that companies use.[4] But it is important to keep in mind that the assumption that future demand will resemble past sales can and will fail frequently: New products get introduced that cannibalize sales of existing products, competitors cut prices to gain market share, economies fall into recession, and products experience sudden quality failures.

Since this assumption—that the future will resemble the past—is what justifies the use of past sales to generate a future forecast, it is important to have a forecasting process that distinguishes the case in which this assumption has a high likelihood of holding true and those circumstances where it is likely to be violated. In the former situation, the forecasting process will rely heavily on past sales. For companies that are just embarking on taking forecasting seriously, it is this process to focus on first, since it is the easiest to get right. In the latter case, you need a forecast process that does not rely largely or at all on past sales.

There are two situations in which the use of past sales to project future demand is problematic: new products and end-of-life products. As a general rule, products that are neither new nor end of life—so-called stable products—are those that are amenable to forecasting using past sales. In the case of new products, you need to distinguish between two circumstances: the common case in which a new product is introduced to replace an existing product that has characteristics that largely overlap with the existing product (i.e., a product transition) and the rarer case in which a product is introduced that is very different from existing products. The second case is notoriously difficult to forecast; the former case is challenging too, but one can often make use of past sales of the existing product to create a forecast for the new replacement product. The challenge here almost always is one of predicting the rate of uptake of the new product relative to the old—that is, timing of the product transition. And thus the problem of forecasting new replacement products is closely linked to the problem of forecasting end-of-life products. The key to successful forecasting of end-of-life products and replacement products is considering them together, not in isolation.

The forecasting process should be tailored to at least three different categories of products: stable products, transition products consisting of new replacement products and the end-of-life products they are replacing, and new nonreplacement products. In trying to get a good forecasting process in place, one should focus first on those products that are easiest to forecast—stable products. The next area of focus should be transition products. The last set of products to focus on—and the one that should receive the least attention from a forecasting perspective—is new nonreplacement products. Challenges associated with forecasting these different categories of products are discussed in the following sections.

Forecasting Stable Products

Consider the case of forecasting the future demand of a particular stock-keeping unit (SKU) in a particular sales region. The typical steps in the forecasting process are as follows:

1. Obtain or update historical sales (in units) of the item.
2. Cleanse the historical sales to remove noise due to predictable events—most notably, sales due to promotional events—and to address issues like stock-outs.
3. Apply a statistical method to the historical sales to obtain a forecast.
4. Review the statistical forecast and adjust based on information not reflected in the historical sales—for example, known new or lost accounts, upcoming promotional events, customer input, and so on.
5. Review and publish the final unconstrained forecast and forecast-accuracy metrics.

This process is sound as far as it goes, but many important and difficult issues arise at every step, which make it hard to carry out in practice, particularly when it needs to be repeated on a weekly or monthly basis across thousands, and possibly millions, of SKU-location combinations.

Obtain or Update Historical Sales of the Item

This seems like a straightforward step but isn't. One question that arises is, should you look at order receipt date or the requested order ship date? The former reflects when the order was placed by the customer, but the latter reflects when the customer wants the order shipped. As a general rule, since you are trying to estimate unconstrained demand, the record of historical sales should be as close as possible to the unconstrained demand picture as possible. This means looking at when the order is received from the customer, not when it ships, looking at the requested quantity, not the shipped quantity. But care must be taken depending on how information like this is collected and stored within the information systems of a company. Sometimes customers place orders every day. If the order is not filled, the same order is placed the next day and so on until the order is filled. In this case, using the requested order quantity may significantly overstate demand. Often the requested ship date is automatically populated as some fixed lead time after the order is received and does not truly reflect when the customer wants the order shipped. At other times, the requested ship date is a long time after the order receipt date and does accurately reflect when the customer wants the product shipped. Understanding what the customer is requesting is the challenge here. Often, the data alone cannot tell you the answer. Rather, understanding how the data are collected and how they are populated in the system is key to understanding the best way to measure customer demand.

Another question that arises is, should you count returns—that is, should sales be net of returns, or should they exclude returns? This is a surprisingly difficult question to answer uniformly. For businesses where returns represent a significant fraction of sales, for example, greater than 5% of sales—as is the case for textbook publishers and musical instrument rental companies, to give just two examples—there should be a separate forecast process for returns. That is, demand should be forecasted using gross sales, and returns should be forecasted using historical returns. The most appropriate approach for forecasting returns will likely be different from the approach for forecasting demand. For example, returns are likely highly correlated to the quantity of past sales during a particular period and to the typical time lag between sales and returns, a relationship that can often be exploited in generating the returns forecast.

For other businesses, where returns represent a small fraction of sales, it usually makes sense to exclude returns from past sales, which means that the forecast generated from past sales data will not reflect returns. If the company needs a forecast of returns in these cases, you can usually obtain a reasonable estimate by dividing past returns by past sales (over a reasonable, recent time period) and multiplying this percent by the forecasted demand. There are two practical reasons for excluding returns from past sales: (a) It prevents the sales history from being negative, which may cause problems with statistical forecasting methods, and

(b) it allows returns to be called out separately from forecasted demand, which is often operationally useful. For example, the organization handling reverse logistics will likely want to know the forecast for returns, and if the returns are estimated as a percent of sales, it is easy to generate a returns forecast from the demand forecast.

If returns are included in the past sales, users of the forecast should clearly understand that the forecast generated using net sales will reflect future demand net of returns. In this case, when computing forecast accuracy, actual sales should be netted against returns before comparing to the forecast.

Cleanse the Historical Sales to Remove Noise Due to Predictable Events

This is arguably the most important step in the forecasting process. Yet it is often overlooked or done poorly. If the use of past sales is being used to predict future demand, it follows that the past sales should exclude sales that are not likely to be repeated in the future.[5] The most common errors in practice are not correcting past sales for the effects of promotions and misadjusting sales when stock-outs occur.

An auto supply parts distributor has weekly promotions of different products. Predictably, sales tend to spike on weeks that the promotions occur, followed by a lull in sales in subsequent weeks.[6] The purchasing system has no automated way to forecast promotions nor to adjust sales for promotions (a process sometimes referred to as "depromoting sales") after they occur. As a result, the purchasing personnel have to manually override the purchasing system whenever promotions occur, a process that leads to frequent errors, the most common being forgetting to buy sufficient inventory in anticipation of the promotion and purchasing large quantities after the promotion is over in response to the spike in demand caused by the promotion.

Figure 2.1 shows a case in which sales in week 12 reflect a promotion that occurred during that week. The challenge is figuring out how much of these sales were due to the promotion occurring that week, how much were due to normal sales that would have occurred even if the promotion had not occurred, and how much may have been due to seasonal effects that could be predicted through seasonal patterns. Another related

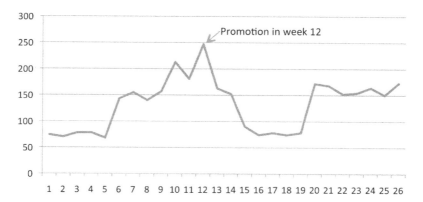

Figure 2.1. Sales of an SKU over a 26-week period. A promotion occurred in week 12. How much of the sales in week 12 were due to the promotion?

challenge is whether subsequent (or prior) sales should be adjusted upward to reflect the fact that the promotion may have had the effect of pulling demand forward (or pushing demand back) rather than of taking market share from other brands or competitors. Specifically, if the promotion had not occurred, demand in weeks 13–19 (or 8–11) may have been higher than what was observed. On the other hand, sales in weeks 15–19 are typically weak due to seasonality. This is not an easy problem to solve. There is no magic formula that will tell you precisely how to decompose the sales in week 12 into its constituent parts: the fraction of sales that would have occurred in week 12 if the promotion had not taken place, the fraction of sales that would have shifted to later or earlier weeks if the promotion had not occurred, and the remaining fraction of organic sales that occurred as a result of carrying out the promotion.

One statistical approach to answering this question is to analyze historical data on a large number of similar promotions to obtain estimates of how to decompose sales during promotion periods. The challenge here is twofold: (a) how to classify promotions and (b) what is the specific algorithm for estimating the sales decomposition based on the promotion sales history. These are both technically difficult problems and worthy of attention in companies where promotions are a frequent occurrence. No commercially available demand planning software solution solves this problem well in an automated fashion. As a result, this step in the demand planning process requires a fair degree of manual intervention to get right. Regardless of how automated the approach is, however, without a process to adjust sales both in anticipation of a promotion and after a promotion occurs, forecasting results using past sales will be poor.

Adjusting sales when stock-outs occur has similar challenges. In Figure 2.2, sales in weeks 12–13 were low because of an inventory stock-out that occurred in the middle of week 12 and lasted until the first couple of days in week 14. The spike in sales in week 14 may have been partially due to pent-up demand. If the sales are left as is, the forecast based on these sales may underestimate demand in weeks 12 and 13. The challenge is how to adjust sales upward during weeks 12–13 (and possibly downward for week 14) to account for the stock-out. The usual approach is to estimate what the sales would have been if a stock-out had not occurred and adjust the sales upward to this normal sales level. The difficulty is how to operationalize this without making some obvious mistakes. When estimating what sales would have been, it is tempting to look at sales in proximate periods in which stock-outs did not occur. This can often lead to overestimates of sales. In the case of using periods prior to the stock-out, one needs to take care that the stock-out was not caused by a spike in demand during prior periods (some of which may have been due to demand shifted backward from future periods). On the other hand, using periods after the stock-out occurs can lead to overestimates of demand because the sales in these periods may have been due to

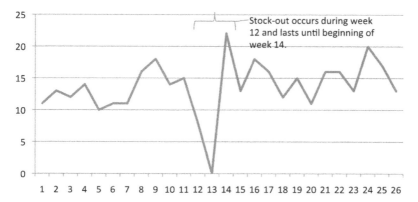

Figure 2.2. Sales of an SKU over a 26-week period. How should sales be adjusted in weeks 12–14 when a stock-out occurred?

pent-up or backlogged demand caused by the stock-out. Another subtle challenge is how to handle partial stock-outs: In this example, since the stock-out occurred in the middle of week 12, the effect on sales in week 12 was weaker than in week 13, which incurred a stock-out during the entire week. In this case, the sales in week 12 would need to be adjusted by a smaller amount than those in week 13.

Apply a Statistical Method to the (Cleansed) Historical Sales to Obtain a Forecast

Entire books are devoted to this step, and dozens of software packages are available that perform this with varying levels of sophistication.[7] The majority of methods utilized are variants of the following procedure:

1. Estimate a baseline value (i.e., a y-intercept), which is a theoretical estimate of current sales without adjusting for a trend or seasonality.
2. Estimate a trend, which might be a linear or a nonlinear, usually exponentially decaying, slope.
3. Estimate seasonality indices for each period over a defined cycle, usually one year. If the forecast is generated in monthly increments, there will be 12 seasonal indices, one for each month. If the forecast is generated in weekly increments, there will 52 seasonal indices.
4. Combine the baseline, trend, and seasonality indices to obtain a forecast. There are two common ways to do this: (a) a multiplicative approach whereby the seasonality indices multiply the baseline and trend and (b) an additive approach whereby the seasonality, baseline, and trend are added together. Specifically, if we position ourselves at the beginning of period t and wish to construct a forecast for demand i periods ($i = 0, 1, 2, \ldots$) in the future, the multiplicative approach will look like

$$f(t + i, t) = (b + m(i)) * S(t + i),$$

where b is the baseline estimate obtained in step 1, $m(i)$ is the trend estimate for i periods in the future obtained in step 2, and $S(t + i)$ is the seasonality index determined for period $t + i$ in step 3. The additive approach looks like the following:

$$f(t + i,t) = b + m(i) + S(t + i).$$

It should be emphasized that the values for the seasonality indices will be different depending on whether an additive or multiplicative approach is utilized in step 4.

A variety of approaches have been developed to estimate the baseline, trend, and seasonality indices in steps 1–3. Linear regression is commonly used as is the Holt-Winters method. Details of step 4 can vary, but the biggest distinction is the choice between a multiplicative and additive approach for applying seasonality indices. The two approaches can give strikingly different results, as can be seen in Figure 2.3, where two 26-week forecasts generated from the same underlying 2 years of historical sales data are displayed. The approach using multiplicative seasonality in this case forecasts much more pronounced seasonal sales effects than the additive seasonality method. From a practical perspective, the multiplicative approach is easier to maintain over time because the seasonal indices are scale invariant, meaning that they can be applied across a variety of SKUs that share the same seasonality profile, even if the demand for the SKUs varies significantly. As a result, a relatively small number of seasonality profiles can be maintained and applied to a large number of SKUs.

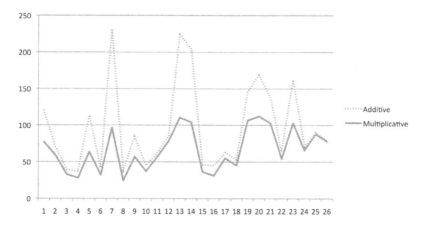

Figure 2.3. Additive and multiplicative seasonality forecasts based on the same historical sales data. In this case, the multiplicative approach forecasts much more pronounced seasonality effects than the additive approach.

Many variants of this four-step procedure for generating a statistical forecast have been proposed. One modification is to impose other cyclical factors, besides seasonality, on the forecast. This amounts to having multiple seasonal factors at work, each based on a specific periodicity. Rarely does introducing additional cyclical factors do much to improve forecasting accuracy, though if there is specific knowledge about the presence of multiple forms of cyclicality, then exploiting this knowledge may be warranted.

Autoselection: An Approach for Selecting a Statistical Forecast Method

Given the plethora of statistical approaches for generating a forecast from past sales, the obvious question is, which methods give rise to the most accurate forecasts? Forecasting experts engage in fierce debates and competitions about what statistical forecasting methods are most effective.[8] Not surprisingly, no consensus has emerged on what methods perform best. There is not even an agreed on practical framework that indicates the most promising methods based on product attributes. Rather than arguing the theoretical merits of different methods, I recommend using an empirical approach called "autoselection" for sorting out which methods work best for which SKUs. Specifically, the autoselection approach leverages the power of computers to analyze performance of many different methods on actual historical sales data and lets performance dictate which methods are selected. Until recently, such an approach was not practical on a large scale because of limits on computing power and storage.[9]

These days, the approach is eminently practical and affordable, so much so that most forecasting software solutions offer variants on the autoselection approach. Unfortunately, the implementation of this approach is often poor. In one case, a software-vendor consultant involved in the implementation of their solution with a client recommended not using their autoselection algorithm because it led to unstable behavior: The method would often oscillate between different forecasting methods from one period to the next, leading to forecasts that changed dramatically from period to period. When the implementation consultant employed by a software company recommends avoiding the use of a key feature of its software, that is a sure sign of poor software design.

In this case, the problem is not with the concept of an autoselection approach but with how the autoselection method is implemented.

The use of an autoselection procedure does not obviate the need for human involvement in the generation of a statistical forecast. The procedure requires careful monitoring to ensure that it is working properly, that parameters are set correctly, and that the forecast methods selected make sense. It is intended for the situation in which hundreds of thousands of different SKU locations are being forecasted regularly, and it is not feasible to have a knowledgeable person decide for each item which forecasting method to utilize. In this kind of situation, which occurs frequently in practice, a well-tuned autoselection algorithm can be invaluable.

Key Features of a Robust Autoselection Algorithm

1. *Allow the user to specify what forecast accuracy metric should be utilized to compare different forecasting methods.* Options should include the usual types of metrics—Mean Absolute Percentage Error and Mean Squared Error, as well as variants of these. More important, the user should be able to specify over what period the metrics should be applied: for example, performance of the forecast for predicting cumulative sales 3 months ahead over the last 12 months or an average of predicting sales over 1, 2, and 3 months ahead over the last 6 months.

2. *Allow the user to specify thresholds for when and how often the best forecasting method is changed.* For example, if the current best method is outperformed by another method by more than 3% over 6 periods in a row, then change the best method to the new best method.

3. *Allow the user to specify a large number of different forecasting methods to track among the set of possible statistical methods.* This means not only allowing the user to select among different methods like simple exponential smoothing, Winter-Holt, or an autoregressive integrated moving average (ARIMA) model but also specifying for example, that five different simple exponential smoothing models should be tracked, each with a different smoothing factor or that a moving average model should be tracked with five different seasonality profiles applied. Also, a user should be able to include aggregation methods in the set of autoselection forecasting methods.

One can see how this can easily give rise to thousands of different forecasting methods that are tracked over time.

4. *Allow no unfair bias when selecting the best method by optimizing parameters of statistical methods over the historical sales data.* Some implementations of the autoselection method will determine the optimal parameters for a given method—say, simple exponential smoothing—by finding the parameter that best fits the entire sales history (without withholding some data from the end of the series, sometimes referred to as a holdout set), thus making the method appear to perform much better than it will in practice. In some circles, this is known as cheating.

5. *Allow reporting of the accuracy of the top and runner-up methods over time.* This allows users to gain valuable knowledge about which methods tend to perform better for which sets of SKUs.

6. *Allow various ways to initialize the autoselection method.* The ideal solution would perform back-testing of different methods on historical sales data and present the test results to the user to help determine which method to initially select. At the very least, users should have the ability to select the initial method to be utilized.

Several demand planning software solutions with which I have worked unfortunately do not implement many of these autoselection features. As a result, deploying a robust autoselection procedure may require development of a custom solution, possibly integrated with your existing demand planning solution.

To Aggregate or Not to Aggregate?

A variant of the following question often arises when generating a statistical forecast based on historical sales: At what level of the product, geography, or time hierarchy is it best to forecast?

- If a company needs to generate a forecast at the SKU-warehouse level but the SKU is sold through many warehouses, is it preferable to first generate a forecast based on sales across all warehouses and then decompose this forecast down to the warehouse level? Or is it better to generate the forecast directly at the warehouse level to begin with?

- If a company needs a forecast for a specific component that is utilized in many products, is it better to forecast the demand for the component by forecasting the sales of all the products that utilize the component and then add up the resulting forecasts (and multiplying by bill of material usage) to obtain the component-level forecast? Or should the forecast be generated by looking at the historical sales of the component across all products and generating a forecast directly from this history?
- If a company needs a forecast for a specific SKU, is it better to first generate a forecast for the product family to which the SKU belongs based on aggregate sales of the product family and then disaggregate the forecast to the SKU level? Or is it preferable to generate the forecast based on SKU-specific sales?
- If a company needs a forecast for an SKU in weekly increments for one year, is it better to generate a forecast for the entire year based on prior year sales and then decompose this forecast into weekly increments using a seasonality profile? Or is it better to generate the forecast in weekly increments based on weekly historical sales?

At the heart of all of these related questions is the abstract question: Does it ever pay to aggregate historical sales data, generate a statistical forecast based on the aggregate sales, and then disaggregate the resulting forecast? Or are we better off generating a statistical forecast based on historical sales at the level at which the forecast is needed? There is no single right answer. Much depends on the nature of demand—for example, how correlated demands are among the aggregated products—and how disaggregation of an aggregate forecast is done. Figure 2.4 shows a contrived example of sales for five products. The aggregate sales for these five products for each period is always the same—625 units. So forecasting at an aggregate level will result in a highly accurate forecast—625 units. This fact surely should be exploited in generating a forecast at the individual product level—whatever forecasts are generated, it should be the case that the forecasts should sum to 625 units per period. But the question remains: Should we start with the aggregate forecast of 625 units per period and apply a method to disaggregate the forecast to obtain forecasts for each of the five

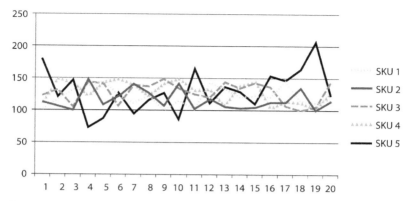

Figure 2.4. Contrived example of sales of five SKUs. Sum of sales of all units in each period is 625 units. Forecasting the aggregate sales for all five SKUs is easy, but disaggregating the forecast to the SKU level is hard.

products? Or should we generate forecasts for each of the five products and then normalize the resulting forecasts so that they sum to 625 units?

Unfortunately, very little assistance in the form of good research is available to help answer this question. From a theoretical perspective, we might be tempted to argue that it does not matter: Because the same information is available to the forecaster whether he or she is forecasting at an aggregate or detailed level, we can plausibly argue that the forecaster can achieve a forecast accuracy no better or worse in the long run via aggregation. This may or may not be true, but there remains the practical challenge of how best to disaggregate an aggregate forecast. Demand planning software packages usually allow users to forecast at an aggregate level and offer ways to disaggregate forecasts but don't generally offer guidance about which methods work best. The most common form of disaggregation is based on proportionality and uses a window of past sales to determine the proportionality factors. For instance, one might take a moving average of the most recent six periods of sales history and determine the proportionality factors by dividing the moving averages for each product by the sum of the moving averages across all products in the aggregation. The aggregate forecast then would be multiplied by these proportionality factors to obtain the disaggregated forecasts.

The bottom line is that aggregation methods should be considered as serious candidates in forecasting and the autoselection algorithm described earlier should include at least some aggregation methods in the set of methods that are tracked. However, there is no guarantee that aggregation methods will outperform more direct forecasting methods.

Beware of Trends

Detecting a linear trend in historical sales using regression or some other method and projecting that trend out over more than a short period of time is almost always a mistake. In practice, methods that estimate and apply a linear trend tend to perform poorly. There is often so much noise in the sales data that the trend is easily over- or underestimated. Applying the misestimated trend to forecasts more than one or two periods in the future greatly amplifies the effect of the error in the estimate. One solution is to apply a damped trend, but the problem then is determining what the damping factor should be. There is no easy solution here, but there is a possible solution if the autoselection procedure described earlier is utilized: Have at least one forecasting method that utilizes no trend. This way, if the trends are badly estimated, the methods that utilize trends will underperform those without trend.

Slow Selling and Intermittent Demand

The much observed rule that ~20% of SKUs account for ~80% of sales means that a large number of items that a company sells are slow sellers. Figure 2.5 shows the sales history for some typical slow-selling items. In case A, the item usually sells in the range of 0–10 units per period. In case B, long periods of zero sales are punctuated with a few periods with spikes of 10–20 units sold. In case C, sales are often zero, but sales of a small number of units occur regularly. These kinds of situations present special challenges to the forecaster. Some specialized statistical methods may work well here. One such approach is to assume the demand is generated from a compound Poisson process and to estimate the parameters of the process from historical sales data. It is not clear, however, that such methods work any better than more standard statistical methods, unless there is some underlying reason to believe the demand is being generated from such a process.[10]

Should forecasts for slow sellers be allowed to be fractional, even if the product can be sold only in integer quantities? In general, the answer

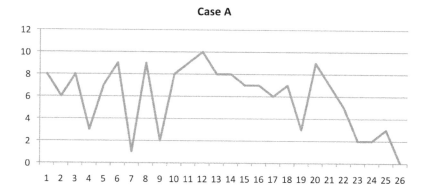

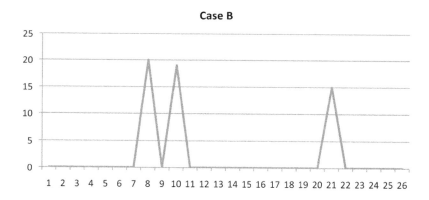

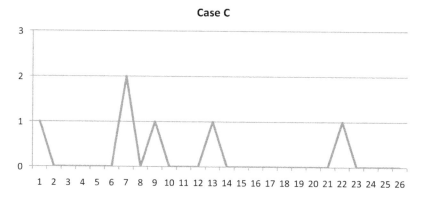

Figure 2.5. Three prototypical examples of slow sellers.

is yes. Forcing the forecast to take on integer values can lead to unnecessarily poor forecasts. In case C, for example, a forecast of 0.25 units per period is likely preferable to a forecast of three zeros followed by a one. In both cases, the average forecast per period is 0.25 units, but in the second case, unless there are concrete reasons to believe that the sale of one unit is going to occur in a particular period, it may lead to decisions that place too much faith on the period in which the demand is forecasted to occur. For example, a purchasing system that looks 3 weeks into the future to decide how much inventory to purchase would decide to stock 0 units if the forecast for the next 3 weeks was 0. If the forecast was 0.25 units, however, the forecasting system would see a demand of 0.75 units, rather than 0, and might decide to stock one or more units.[11] This could lead to the difference between a sale and a lost sale.

Maintaining Seasonality Indices

One of the major drawbacks of some statistical methods incorporating seasonality—most notably, the Holt-Winters triple exponential smoothing method—is that in the usual implementation, the seasonality factors are maintained for each SKU. This is OK if there is adequate historical data for the SKU to make a reasonable statistical estimate of the seasonal factors. However, in practice, this is frequently not the case. In many situations, having more than one year of historical data to use for estimating seasonal factors is out of the question, and most practical guides for using Holt-Winters suggest having at least 3 years of historical data. Even if 3 years of data are available, there are only 3 data points on which to base the estimate of each seasonal index, hardly a statistically significant sample. Also, the product may have undergone significant changes in its sales patterns over the 3 years, so that treating the 3 years as three 1-year sets of independent samples is suspect.

This raises the question then of whether it is really reasonable in practice to maintain seasonal indices for individual SKUs. In most cases, the answer is no. Rather, it is much more reasonable to maintain a set of seasonality indices, each of which is utilized for different sets of SKUs and geographical sales regions. If you are using the autoselection algorithm, you can have multiple seasonality profiles competing against each other to determine the best seasonality profile for a given SKU.

Managing seasonality profiles requires some initialization steps and some maintenance activities. The initialization steps include deriving an initial set of seasonality indices and assigning a set of seasonality indices to SKUs. Maintenance activities include updating seasonality indices over time to incorporate new data and changed circumstances, reassigning seasonality indices to SKUs, and assigning seasonality indices to new SKUs.

To create an initial set of seasonality profiles, decide first how many seasonality profiles are appropriate by figuring out the different kinds of seasonality that affect sales of products. The number should be as small as possible. A half dozen is reasonable in most cases and certainly not more than around 20. As a first step, describe the different kinds of seasonal effects that drive your business. You may have products that tend to sell more in the summer months and others that sell in winter months. You may have products that are sold primarily around certain holidays and others that sell steadily throughout the year. Some products may have a pronounced seasonal profile in one geographical region and quite a different profile in another. This initial segmentation of products can be modified over time so getting it exactly right at first is not critical. A luxury goods company uses approximately 50 seasonal profiles in their global forecasting process. There are about seven different profiles per geographic region, one for each product category. Figure 2.6 shows the seasonality profiles for five product categories in Asia for 2008. Virtually all the seasonality profiles have a significant spike in December due to end-of-year holiday sales. Product category 5 is for winter clothing and has particularly heavy sales through the fall. Product category 2 has seasonality indices in January through March that are high as well, due to the fact that sales in this category are elevated due to the Chinese New Year. Since the Chinese New Year is a lunar holiday and can fall in different months, the seasonality indices need to be updated each year to reflect when the holiday occurs.

Once you have decided on an initial set of seasonality profiles, perform an initial assignment of existing SKUs to the seasonality profiles. If there is some question about how to assign an SKU to a profile, don't assign it. At the end of this exercise, each seasonality profile should have an initial set of at least a few dozen, and possibly thousands, of SKUs assigned to it.

The next step is to determine an initial set of seasonality indices for each profile. This requires collecting sales data that has been cleansed of

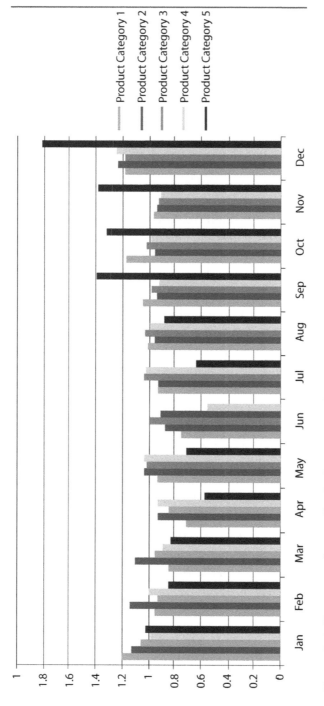

Figure 2.6. Five seasonality profiles for forecasting sales in Asia.

nonrepeating promotional events and adjusted for stock-outs. Though the details for calculating an initial set of indices for a profile can vary, the procedure should look something like the following, where we are assuming that seasonality indices are being determined for each month of the calendar year:

1. Divide the data into individual complete 1-year observation sets. This means that if sales data exist for an SKU for 2.5 years, take 2 complete calendar years of data (discarding the remaining data), and break these 2 years into two 1-year sets, with the first element of each series corresponding to the first month (January) of the calendar year.

2. Normalize each 1-year observation set by dividing each value by the mean of the observation set.

3. Perform a linear regression across all observations for the seasonality profile using dummy variables for each month (excluding one) as the independent variables. The results of the regression analysis (R-squared and p-values) should be examined to determine significance. Assuming the results are satisfactory, the coefficients obtained from this regression should serve as an initial set of seasonality indices.

If the results of the regression in step 3 are unsatisfactory, go back to the original data and ensure that the set of SKUs being included reflect the appropriate seasonality. If not, remove these SKUs from the data set and repeat the analysis. If you feel the data are correct and the regression results are still unsatisfactory, one choice is to simply not use seasonality indices for this set of SKUs.

In the previously described procedure, no mention is made of removing a trend from the historical sales data. You may decide to include a trend in the regression in step 3—but it is not necessary. Including a trend factor can lead to dampened estimates of seasonality effects, so proceed with care if using a trend factor.

If seasonality profiles are needed for forecasting in weekly increments, you have two choices. You can maintain seasonality profiles in monthly values and utilize these when generating forecasts in weekly increments. If a week falls in January, for example, the seasonality index would be the

January index. If the week falls between January and February, you can use a weighted average of the seasonality indices for January and February.

Alternatively, you can generate and maintain seasonal profiles in weekly increments. This has the advantage of being more precise in capturing holiday effects but has two disadvantages from a maintenance perspective. First, holidays do not always fall on the same week each year, so care must be taken in generating and applying the seasonality indices to handle this fact. Second, maintaining 52 values in a seasonal profile, as opposed to 12, requires more effort, particularly if these are being reviewed and adjusted manually.

Maintaining seasonal profiles over time and reassigning SKUs to different profiles require diligence. The tendency is for companies to set them once and rarely, if ever, to review them. This will lead to degraded forecast performance over time. If the autoselection procedure is utilized, the problem of assigning SKUs to seasonality profiles can be largely automated: You simply include a set of different seasonality profiles among the set of defined forecasting methods, and the forecasting method that performs best over time will determine the best seasonality profile (if any) for that SKU. As for maintaining and updating the seasonality profiles themselves, a periodic process of recalculating the seasonality profiles based on recent sales data should be put into place. These new seasonality profiles should not necessarily replace the old ones, but their performance should be compared to the old profiles. At the very least, these new profiles can be included in the profiles considered in the autoselection approach and their performance tracked over time.

Review and Adjust the Statistical Forecast Using Information Not in Historical Sales

This step is perhaps the least understood and poorest executed in the forecasting process. It is poorly executed partially because it is manually intensive. Companies tend to neglect manually intensive processes for the same reason people do: They require work. The step in principal is straightforward: It entails examining the statistical forecast generated in the previous step and deciding whether it should be overridden because of information that was not reflected in the past sales of the item.

Often, adjustments are made by members of the sales department. This is where the first source of error often creeps in. Salespeople are interested in sales. If a forecast for a product does not look like it is consistent with their often rosy view of the future, they will be inclined to adjust the forecast upward. This is not the purpose of this step, and it is the reason this step should not be performed directly by sales personnel but rather by a member of the forecasting group (part of operations, not sales) in consultation with sales.

In general, an adjustment should be made to the forecast only if there is material information available to the company that indicates that the past sales for this product are likely to be a poor gauge of future sales. The most common situations that justify a forecast adjustment are a planned promotion or the adoption or loss of a significant new customer or account. For companies with significant promotion activities, the adjustment of the forecast to reflect additional sales due to a planned promotion is perhaps the most important single step in the entire forecasting process. Significant effort may be justified to create forecasting capabilities to predict the effect of a promotion on sales. For example, it is not unusual for supermarkets to rely on sophisticated regression models to forecast the uplift in sales based on a variety of details surrounding the promotion: where the item appears in an advertising circular, the distribution of the circular, the amount by which the item is being discounted, and so on. Because many of the adjustments to the forecast that occur in this step must be made manually, the step can be overwhelming for companies that may be managing tens of thousands of SKUs. This is one of the major challenges companies must deal with. There is no easy solution. Ideally, a forecaster would review every statistical forecast generated and make informed judgments to adjust these based on the latest information available. This is obviously not possible in most cases, so some process must be found to try to bring the most likely candidates for adjustment to the attention of the forecasting personnel in an automated fashion. Demand planning software solutions refer to this capability as "management by exception." It is easy enough to implement a system that brings to the user's attention the SKUs that need to be reviewed based on a well-defined filter. The challenge is defining the filter in a meaningful way. How do you automatically identify which, of the tens of thousands of items that are being forecasted, should be reviewed by forecast personnel? And how do you do this in such a way that the number of exceptions does not overwhelm the forecast personnel?

One approach is to highlight those items that have historically poor forecast accuracy. This can be automated but can often result in many false positives: a large number of items brought to the attention of the forecaster that have poor forecast accuracy but whose forecast should not be modified. Another approach is to proactively identify those items that are likely to be affected by a new or lost customer. But this approach to some extent begs the question because it requires information about new or lost customers, as well as the products these customers are likely to order to be entered into the demand planning system so that it can then flag these items for review. If this information is not being entered in a timely fashion, this approach will fail.

Another promising approach is to highlight those items that have been significantly and consistently over- or underforecasted, as measured by forecast bias. Defining what is meant by "significantly and consistently" in this context depends on a number of factors and may change over time. A reasonable starting definition is that if a forecast for an item has been over- or underforecasted in more than 75% of the last six cycles by an average of more than 50%, then it should be considered as significantly and consistently over- or underforecasted, and the item should be flagged for review. Often, in these cases, a root cause analysis will reveal a systematic error in the forecasting process that needs to be corrected.

Any adjustments made to the forecast in this step of the process should result in a new forecast that should be tracked separately from the forecast generated in the previous step. The reason is obvious: While adjustments may be made with the best of intentions, it is not at all clear that such adjustments improve forecast accuracy. By tracking both the unadjusted and adjusted forecast, you can determine over time whether these adjustments are helping or hurting forecast accuracy.

Role of Customer Forecast Collaboration

One way in which material information affecting future demand can be surfaced is through direct communication with key customers, who may have knowledge about their future demand needs that is not reflected in past sales. Customer forecast collaboration is the term used to refer to the process of obtaining information from customers about the forecast.

Forecast collaboration with a customer will require the generation of a forecast at the individual customer level, either to share with the customer or to compare with the forecast provided by the customer. If the forecasts being generated in the previous step are not being generated at the individual customer level, an additional step in the forecasting process will be required to decompose the forecast to the individual customer level.

Sometimes customers initiate the forecast collaboration process by sharing their forecast with their suppliers with the expectation that by providing a view of their likely demand, they will obtain improved or preferential service. The forecast obtained from customers should be viewed skeptically. It is often inflated because they want the suppliers to be prepared for the best case scenario, not the most likely one. Reconciling the forecast from the customer with the internally generated forecast is a necessary first step in determining whether the internal forecast should be adjusted. If the difference between the internal forecast and the customer forecast is significant, then a truly collaborative process will involve discovering the root cause of the discrepancy. If, at the end of this process, there is reason to believe that the customer forecast captures new information that is not reflected in the internal forecast, then an adjustment to the forecast may be warranted. But care should be taken not to take customer claims at face value. For example, a customer might claim that demand is going to increase because of market share gains that they are anticipating. Even if this is true, it may not result in overall higher demand for your company if the competitors of this customer (from whom market share is presumably going to be taken) are customers of yours as well.

If a customer has not initiated a collaboration process with you and you wish to begin one with them, the best first step is to share your forecast with the customer and request specific feedback about whether the forecast should be modified or not.

In recent years, many software tools have appeared that enable various types of collaboration with customers and suppliers, usually through a web interface. Such tools are valuable in certain domains, but in the context of customer forecast collaboration, they generally do not encourage meaningful collaboration. Rather, they tend to enable sharing of the forecasts only, not a deeper understanding about why the forecasts may differ, which will likely occur only as a result of conversations between knowledgeable parties at the companies. Such discussions should become a regular part of any meaningful customer forecast collaboration process.

Review and Publish the Final Unconstrained Forecast and Forecast Accuracy Metrics

The generation of an unconstrained forecast is an important first step in planning for future demand. In many cases, though, before it can be utilized by production, procurement, and other personnel, it needs to be transformed into what is often referred to as a sales and operations plan. This transformation—which is the focus of the S&OP process—is the critical next step in the supply chain planning process. As a result, the unconstrained forecast by itself is not usually something that other functions within a company need direct access to. However, there are several direct uses to which the unconstrained forecast and forecast accuracy metrics should be put:

- The unconstrained forecast can be compared to the revenue targets for the company to get an early warning on whether there is a significant disconnect.
- The forecast accuracy metrics can be examined to identify where problems exist and understand where improvements in the forecasting process should be made. In particular, bias metrics can be utilized to identify items that are significantly and consistently over- or underforecasted. These items can then be examined in detail to understand and correct the problems that are driving the forecast errors.
- The forecast accuracy metrics can be utilized to estimate underlying demand variability, which can be utilized in S&OP and inventory and supply planning.
- Comparison of the performance of different statistical approaches can be performed to understand which methods appear to be working best.

In general, not enough time is spent by companies looking at the results of the forecasting process, understanding them, and taking actions to improve the process. In most cases, the process ends with the generation of the unconstrained forecast with barely a glance at the forecast accuracy metrics. As a result, opportunities for improvement are not realized.

Forecasting Transition Products: New Products Replacing End-of-Life Products

Forecasting end-of-life products and the products that are replacing them is tricky because of the many difficult-to-predict factors that affect product transitions. Sometimes product transitions need to be altered at the last minute because of manufacturing delays, or competitor actions. Sometimes companies announce the new product to much fanfare, but customers react with a shrug, or worse, with resistance to the new product. A large computer manufacturer often struggles with product transitions because customers are not necessarily ready to make a transition to a new product even though the manufacturer has announced its availability. As a result, the transition eventually occurs but takes much longer than projected. Components for the old product need to be chased down to support unanticipated continued demand for the old product while components for the new product remain unused in inventory, losing value quickly.

A textbook publisher wrestles with the challenge of regularly introducing new versions of textbooks. The new textbook is usually just a revision of the previous version and is intended to replace the older version. In principle, the transition is very predictable: The publisher announces a publication date for the new volume, and after that date, the publisher accepts orders only for the new book. In practice, the transition never occurs so smoothly. Figure 2.7 shows the sales of a new textbook and those of an older version it is replacing. The new version was published on July 1, 2010. Its sales ramped up with the fall semester, but the old textbook continued to sell at significant volume as well. In this case, two factors were driving the continued sale of the older version. First, some teachers were requesting that the older version be kept available because they preferred it to the new version. And second, the company owned a significant quantity of inventory of the older version from its last print run.

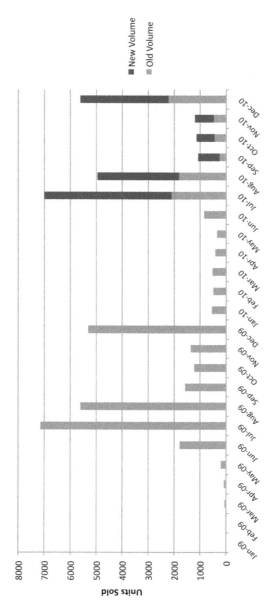

Figure 2.7. Sales of two versions of the same textbook. The new volume appeared in July 2010.

As a general rule, statistical methods based on past sales are not particularly good at forecasting end-of-life and new product sales. In these cases, not enough information is embedded in past sales to provide a reasonable chance for these methods to work. In almost all cases, the best forecasting results will be obtained if someone who is knowledgeable about the products and the transition helps to generate the forecast. Often, the problem is not so much in forecasting the total sales of the new product plus the old product but in forecasting the timing of the transition from old to new. In the textbook example in Figure 2.7, total sales of the old textbook plus the new one remain relatively stable from one year to the next. Applying statistical forecasting methods to the end-of-life product and the new product independently will likely lead to poor results. But a viable alternative procedure utilizing statistical methods in this situation might look like this:

1. Generate a combined forecast for the end-of-life and new product using a statistical forecasting method.
2. Decompose the combined forecast into separate forecasts for the end-of-life and new product based on a transition profile.

The transition profile in step 2 is a nondecreasing sequence of numbers starting from 0 and ending at 1. Figure 2.8 shows some sample transition profiles. Profile 1 would be appropriate for a gradual product transition, where both products may coexist in the market for an extended period. Profile 2 is less gradual, and profile 3 represents the extreme case of a forced and sudden transition from one product to another.

If this approach is utilized, there are three challenges: defining the transition profiles, assigning a profile to a given pair of products, and figuring out the timing of when the transition is going to occur. The process for maintaining and assigning transition profiles is similar to the process outlined for seasonality profiles. The first step is to define an initial set of transition profiles by looking at sales history for past product transitions. This should give rise to a small (probably no more than ~5–10) set of transition profiles. Then someone must decide which transition profile to apply for an upcoming product transition and when to apply the profile. This is a decision that should not be left to a software system to automatically make. In fact, this is most likely a decision that should be made as

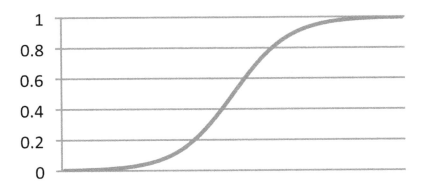

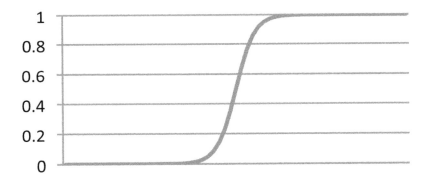

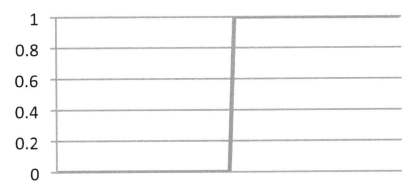

Figure 2.8. Possible transition profiles for decomposing the combined forecast of an end-of-life product and new product that is replacing it.

part of the S&OP process since it is something that is largely influenced by decisions made within the company—for example, decisions about setting the general availability date for the new product and setting the cutoff date for accepting orders for the old product.

Assessing the forecast accuracy for product transitions should look at both the overall forecast for the combined end-of-life and new product (from step 1), as well as whether the transition profile and timing were accurate.

Customer forecast collaboration can be especially helpful when forecasting transition products, particularly if the transition is heavily affected by the rate of adoption of the new product among a few key customers. In this case, sharing the proposed transition (either the transition profile or the actual customer forecast for the transition products) with a customer will allow you to obtain potentially valuable insight into the readiness of the customer to adopt the new product, possibly resulting in a change to the transition forecast.

Forecasting New Nonreplacement Products

The holy grail of forecasting is predicting the sales of products that are wholly or largely new to the market. This is obviously difficult because past sales of a like product either do not exist or are too unreliable to form the basis of a forecast. Companies sometimes get caught up in trying to find sophisticated statistical models to forecast these products. This is a mistake. Fortunately, these kinds of new product introductions are relatively rare. In these circumstances, statistical models are not likely to yield reliable results, and companies should obtain forecasts through other means—for example, via consensus from sales personnel or through forecast collaboration with customers. Companies should treat these forecasts as highly unreliable and should instead focus on ways to mitigate dependence on the forecast.

One way to mitigate reliance on a forecast is through lead time reduction or other quick response initiatives. Companies in the fashion industry often are faced with the challenge of forecasting demand for products for which reliable past sales do not exist. In these cases, rather than trying to forecast demand accurately, companies are better off focusing attention on how to respond more quickly to demand.[12]

A common idea for forecasting new products is to utilize the initial weeks of new product sales to generate a statistical forecast or to revise the original forecast. This may be effective but may just as often lead companies astray. The first few weeks of sales of a new product may be desultory, indicating to someone looking at the sales that the product is going to be a dog. Then, suddenly, the product takes off. If you react too quickly to initial sales in this case and reduce supplies accordingly, you risk missing significant demand. The reverse case happens too: Initial sales are strong so forecasts are adjusted upward. But subsequent weeks see demand quickly dropping after the initial wave of excitement wears off.

Managing Forecast Category Transitions

We've discussed different forecasting processes to utilize depending on whether a product is stable, new, or in transition. The point of making this distinction is to differentiate those items that are typically not well suited to being forecasted using statistical methods because their past sales are not a good indicator of future demand. If we have different forecasting processes to handle these different product categories, the challenge arises about how to identify which products belong to which category. Specifically, how do you decide which products are stable, whether a stable product is no longer stable, and when a product early in its lifecycle should be considered part of the set of stable products? This is a process that is both difficult to automate and often neglected. The result, over time, is a misaligned forecasting process that results in degraded forecast performance.

One way in which software can help is by monitoring forecast accuracy of different statistical methods over time for *all* items, not just those that are in the set of stable products. For items that are new—both replacement and nonreplacement—the forecast accuracy can be used as a gauge to help flag those items that might be ready to enter the set of stable products. If the forecast accuracy rises above a certain threshold, the software can flag these items for review by forecasting personnel, who can then make the final decision about whether they can be considered stable. Likewise, products beginning to near end of life may start to experience poorer forecast accuracy. If they fall below a certain forecast accuracy threshold, the software can flag these for review to decide if they need to be removed from the set of stable products.

One of the problems with this approach is that because forecast accuracy is a lagging indicator, it may not flag items in a timely fashion. For example, degraded forecast performance for an item entering end of life may not show up in the metrics until well after the items' sales have begun to drop off. It is therefore critical to supplement any automated approach with the kind of knowledge that usually resides only in the heads of knowledgeable sales and forecast personnel.

Forecast Accuracy Metrics

The adage "if it's not measured, it's not managed" is as true of forecasting as any other business activity, and yet many companies either fail to track forecast accuracy or do not report it to senior management in a meaningful way. Even if reports are distributed, rarely do managers spend much time reviewing them because they usually are not actionable. If your overall forecast accuracy is 70%, you might be unhappy (or happy), but the path to getting to 80% is not clear.

Review of Forecast Metrics

Broadly, there are two key metrics that should be reported: forecast accuracy and forecast bias. In many ways, forecast bias is more important to focus on than forecast accuracy because systematic under- or overforecasting is a common problem and will not be exposed by looking at forecast accuracy metrics alone. Most books on forecasting discuss four metrics: mean absolute percentage error (MAPE), mean squared error (MSE), mean percentage error (MPE), and mean absolute deviation (MAD). If the forecast for a period is F and the actual sales for that same period is A, then these metrics are defined as follows:

$$\text{MAPE} = \frac{|F - A|}{A}$$

$$\text{MSE} = (F - A)^2$$

$$\text{MPE} = \frac{F - A}{A}$$

$$\text{MAD} = |F - A|.$$

All these metrics have problems. The MAD and MSE are difficult to use because they do not allow easy comparison across different SKUs with different sales volume. For example, if the forecast for one SKU is 80 and actual sales are 100 while the forecast for another SKU is 8 and actual sales are 10, the MAD for the first SKU is 20 while for the second SKU it is 2. No direct comparison between the first and second case can be made on the basis of the MAD metric. For this reason, in practice, the MAD and MSE metrics are not useful. The MAPE metric attempts to correct this scale issue by normalizing, with respect to actual sales, and expressing the error as a percent of actual sales. The MPE metric is similar to the MAPE metric but is intended to measure forecast bias.

The MAPE metric suffers from the problem of asymmetry: If you forecast 5 and sales are 10, the MAPE metric yields a value of 50%, while if you forecast 10 and sales are 5, the MAPE metric reports an error of 100%. The same is true of the MPE metric. Intuitively, an error metric should report the forecast accuracy in both cases as the same. Another problem with the MAPE metric is that it is theoretically unbounded and becomes undefined when $A = 0$, which can happen frequently, especially with slow-selling items.

Modified versions of the MAPE metric have been proposed to address these problems. One is the following:[13]

$$\text{sMAPE} = \frac{|F - A|}{(|F| + |A|) / 2}.$$

This has the desirable properties that it is bounded (between 0 and 200%), it reports overforecasting and underforecasting by the same absolute magnitude as the same error, and it is defined as long as either F or A is nonzero. However, this metric is somewhat counterintuitive when forecast errors are large. For example, if the forecast is 30 and sales are 100, the sMAPE gives an error of 108%. An alternative modification to the MAPE is possible that avoids this counterintuitive result:[14]

$$\text{mMAPE} = \frac{|F - A|}{max(F, A)}.$$

This metric has the property that it is between 0 and 100% (assuming $F, A \geq 0$ and at least one is > 0). It has the same symmetric property as the sMAPE metric, and it gives intuitive results in most cases. For example, when the forecast is 30 and sales are 100, the mMAPE gives an error of 70%. The mMAPE metric does not perform well if F and A are allowed to be negative, but for most businesses, this situation should not arise in practice.[15]

As a practical reporting metric, therefore, the mMAPE metric is a strong candidate because it is simple and intuitive. Also, a relatively trivial side benefit of using the mMAPE metric for reporting purposes is that instead of reporting forecast error, you can report forecast accuracy as 1– mMAPE expressed as a percent. To some managers, forecast accuracy is more intuitive than forecast error and the 1– mMAPE metric has the intuitive property that when it is reported as 100% (the maximum value), it means the forecast equals the actual sales.

A similar modification to the mean percent error metric is appropriate:

$$\mathrm{mMPE} = \frac{F - A}{max(F, A)} \quad .$$

Over What Horizon Should Forecast Accuracy Be Measured?

When reporting any forecast accuracy metric in practice, two questions arise:

- Over what forecast horizon should the metric be calculated?
- How many observations should be included in calculating the forecast accuracy metric?

To clarify, suppose we are standing at the end of week n and want to calculate a forecast accuracy metric for an SKU. We assume that we have at our disposal the 52-week-ahead forecasts generated at the beginning of weeks 1, 2, . . . n, which we can denote by $F(t, t + i)$, $t = 1, \ldots, n$ and $i = 0, \ldots 51$. For example, $F(3,7)$ is the forecast for week 7 that was generated at the start of week 3—that is, the 4-week-ahead forecast standing at the start of week 3. We also assume we have the actual sales realized in weeks 1, . . . n, denoted by $A(t)$, $t = 1, \ldots, n$. The first question is concerned with what values of i should the metric span over—that is, what look-ahead period is relevant—and the second question is what values of t the metric should cover—that is, which prior forecasts should be included.

Many companies and demand planning software solutions calculate metrics assuming $i = 0$, meaning they look only at 1-week-ahead forecast accuracy. This is valid if the company relies only on the 1-week-ahead forecast, which is almost never the case. Such an approach can give a vastly misleading sense of how well the company is forecasting because of the tendency for forecasts to be more accurate over shorter time horizons. The right approach will vary by company and depends on what period ahead the company typically relies on the forecast. In general, the recommended approach is to choose a range of values for i and report a weighted average of the forecast accuracy over this range of values. For example, suppose your company relies on forecasts up to 12 weeks ahead, but the most important forecast values are for weeks 1–3, followed by weeks 4–6, and then weeks 7–12. A reasonable approach might weight weeks 1–3 at 50% (each week weighted at 16.7%), weeks 4–6 at 25% (each week weighted at 8.3%), and weeks 7–12 at 25% (each week weighted at 4.2%). The mMAPE forecast accuracy for the forecast generated at the start of period t using this weighting scheme would be calculated as

$$\text{mMAPE}(t) = \sum_{i=0}^{11} w_i \frac{\left|F(t,t+i) - A(t+i)\right|}{\max\left(F(t,t+i), A(t+i)\right)},$$

where w_i is the weight given to the i-period ahead forecast. In this example, $w_i = 0.167$ for $i = 0, 1, 2$, $w_i = 0.083$ for $i = 3, 4, 5$, and $w_i = 0.042$ for $i = 6, 7, 8, 9, 10, 11$. An important practical consideration in choosing how large i should be is that the metric calculation can only be done for the forecast generated in week t after i weeks have elapsed. In this example, we can only calculate the metric for the forecast generated 12 or more weeks previous to the current period. For large values of i, this means the accuracy metric will be lagging. It may therefore make sense to report metrics for more than one range of i-values.

There is also the question of what prior forecasts to include in the metric calculation—that is, the range of values of t to consider. In practice, this issue comes down to a tradeoff between responsiveness and robustness. Using the most recent forecast available to perform the metric calculation tells us how well the forecast method is currently doing but leaves us with the question of whether we were just lucky (or unlucky) when that forecast was generated. On the other hand, using a large number of past forecasts in the metric can create the opposite bias: Forecasting methods that performed well in the past will continue to look good even if more recent performance has degraded. In practice, a reasonable compromise is to utilize the most recent three to six forecasts generated. For example, suppose we are at the beginning of week 40 and we wish to calculate the mMAPE(t) forecast metric (with $i = 0, \ldots ,11$) over the most recent three forecasts against which actual sales can be compared. We would utilize the 12-week-ahead forecasts generated at the start of weeks 27, 28, and 29 to calculate the overall forecast metric:

$$\sum_{t=27}^{29} \frac{1}{3} \text{mMAPE}(t) \ .$$

Alternatively, rather than using a straight average, we could use a weighted average where more weight is given to more recent forecasts. Demand planning software solutions generally do not have the flexibility to report metrics of this variety. In order to implement these kinds of metrics in practice, you may need to build the capability yourself—for example, within a data warehouse.

Management Reporting

There is a tendency when providing forecast metrics to upper management to roll up forecasting metrics into a few overall values that summarize forecast accuracy for the entire enterprise. This is often a mistake for two reasons: It masks underlying variability in forecast accuracy, and it makes taking action to improve forecasting difficult. The practical challenge of management reporting of forecasting is twofold: how to summarize forecast accuracy across a large number of SKUs in a way that is meaningful and how to highlight actions that are needed to improve the forecasting process.

Summarizing forecast accuracy in a meaningful way requires knowing how to segment SKUs appropriately, how to summarize forecast accuracy statistics for each segment, and how to clearly identify which SKUs are laggards and which are leaders in forecast accuracy. It is obviously the laggards to which management attention should be given, and identifying root causes for laggard performance and specifying actions to address root causes should be a part of any actionable forecast accuracy report.

Segmenting SKUs for Forecast Accuracy Reporting

Forecast accuracy should be reported based on a logical grouping of SKUs. At the highest level, reporting should be done separately for stable products, transition products (including both end-of-life products and their replacement products, if any), and new nonreplacement products. Further segmentation should be done within each of these categories. The exact segmentation will vary by company but some useful ways to segment results include the following:

- By sales region
- By volume, dividing SKUs into high, medium, and low sales volume
- By product category
- By manufacturing or procurement lead time
- By operating margin or profitability

The most useful way to segment SKUs for reporting forecast accuracy will evolve over time as products change and as drivers of forecast accuracy become better understood.

Calculating Forecast Accuracy Metrics for a Segment of SKUs

A frequent tactical issue that arises when developing management reports for forecasting is how to combine forecast accuracy measures across multiple SKUs into a single overall metric. The first answer is, don't! It is much more useful to display the forecast accuracy across a range of SKUs as a histogram in which the variability of forecast accuracy is easily seen. Looking at forecast accuracy in this way will much more likely lead to productive discussions because attention will naturally be drawn to the relative handful of SKUs whose forecast accuracy is worse (or better) than the group's overall average. Looking at the mean forecast accuracy for the entire segment hides this valuable information.

On the other hand, there is often a need for a summary statistic to report the forecast accuracy for a segment of SKUs. In this case, a straight average of the forecast accuracy metric across all the SKUs is usually not a good choice: It will tend to overweight the items with lower volume. A better choice is a volume weighted metric. For example, to report on the overall mMAPE forecast accuracy defined previously for a group of SKUs, one approach is to calculate the mMAPE metric for a given forecast period t across all SKUs as

$$\text{mMAPE}(t,G) \equiv \sum_{i=0}^{11} w_i \frac{\sum_{g \in G} \left| F_g(t,t+i) - A_g(t+i) \right|}{\sum_{g \in G} \max\left(F_g(t,t+i), A_g(t+i) \right)} \quad ,$$

where the set G is the set of SKUs for which an overall metric is being calculated. Other weighting methods are certainly possible, an obvious choice being simply the actual sales. The next step would be to average this metric over a range of values for t as previously discussed. Volume weighted metrics can be problematic for the opposite reason that the straight average is not desirable: Forecast errors for lower volume SKUs can be overlooked.

To take a simple example, if SKU A has a forecast for 10 and actual sales of 8, while SKU B has a forecast of 50 and actual sales of 100, the mMAPE metric for SKU A alone is 20%, while for SKU B alone it is 50%. The straight average of the metrics gives a value of 35% while the weighted average metric above gives 47%. Which is correct? Both are, but at the same time, both can be misleading and can hide meaningful information. For this reason, summary statistics should form only one part of any forecast accuracy management report.

Measuring and Reporting Forecast Bias

The MPE (or, preferably, the mMPE) metric is sometimes suggested as a metric for forecast bias. The thinking is that over a large set of observations, the mMPE metric should tend to 0% if the forecast is unbiased because you should underforecast as frequently as you overforecast, which should result in canceling out of differences in the numerator. The problem is that, by itself, the MPE metric cannot be easily interpreted. If the mMPE over 20 observations yields a value of 5%, does this mean the forecast is biased or unbiased? A statistical hypothesis test could potentially be applied to help decide whether the value of 5% is significant and in some circumstances, such analysis may be warranted. However, in most cases, companies should really be focused on those situations where there is an obvious forecast bias over a sustained period of time for an identifiable set of SKUs. A bias metric should bring these SKUs to the attention of management in a clear and forceful way.

One way to do this is by graphically reporting the number of SKUs that were over- or underforecasted by more than, say, 25% for more than 80% of the past n forecast periods, where n is a number to be specified based on the amount of forecast history available and other considerations. For example, if $n = 5$, then the report would identify those SKUs that were consistently overforecasted or underforecasted by more than 25% for at least four out of the last five forecasts. Figure 2.9 shows what a sample forecast bias report of this type might look like. This report shows the percent of SKUs by sales volume that have a mean percentage error (MPE) metric within a given range. For this sample report, it is clear at a glance that there is a significant problem with overforecasting and underforecasting for some SKUs. From a management perspective, the next step would be to take a closer look at these SKUs to understand the root causes of the systematic over and underforecasting.

It is also often helpful to provide reports that show the impact of over- and underforecasting. For example, one possibility is to report a scatter plot showing on-hand inventory on one axis and degree of over- and underforecasting on another. This highlights the impact of over- and underforecasting and makes tangible the effect of improving forecast accuracy. Figure 2.10 shows a sample of what a chart like this looks like. Each data point represents a particular part. The x axis plots the mMPE forecast bias metric while the y axis plots the average weeks of supply on hand for the part over a 4-month period. There is a clear correlation between on-hand inventory for the parts and the degree to which the parts have been over- and underforecasted. The data points at either end of the chart correspond to those parts that have significant over- or underforecasting. These parts should be examined more closely

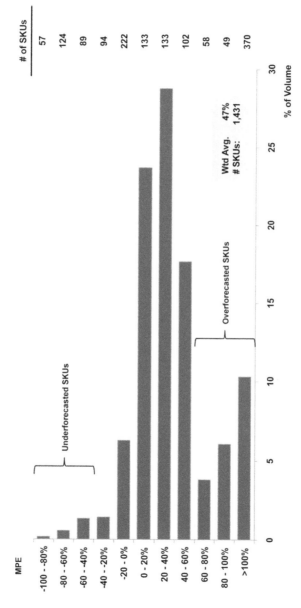

Figure 2.9. Sample forecast bias histogram for a set of SKUs.

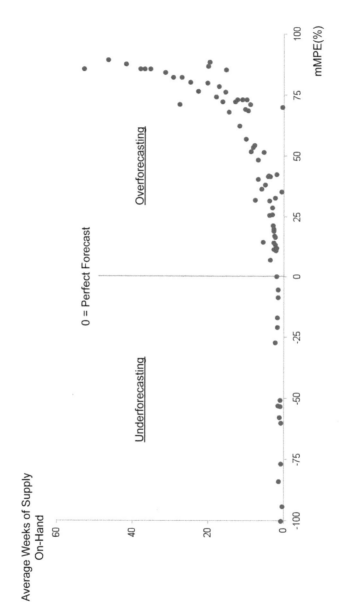

Figure 2.10. Forecast bias versus on-hand inventory for a set of parts.

to understand what is driving the consistent and significant degree of under- and overforecasting.

What Is Achievable? Placing Forecast Accuracy in Context

What is the best possible result in forecasting? Less ambitiously, what is a reasonable objective for a forecasting process? How do you determine that objective, and how do you measure whether you're making progress toward that objective? Any forecast management report needs to answer these questions clearly and concisely.

One of the reasons that forecasting gets short shrift in many companies is that managers view it either as something that cannot be done well or as a mysterious black box about which little is known. If concrete objectives for forecasting are not specified and progress toward those objectives do not materialize, managers are unlikely to spend investment dollars on the activity. The unlucky person on whom it falls in an organization to generate a forecast knows that it is a losing game. The cliché "All forecasts are wrong" doesn't help when it's your forecast that is wrong. That's why the unlucky person in many companies is not a person at all but a computer. It's easy to blame a computer for a bad forecast. By relegating the forecasting process to a black box computer program, managers can absolve themselves of responsibility for its quality.

If forecast accuracy is 70%, who is to say it could not be 80% or 90%? Vendors of demand planning solutions will readily tell you that their solutions will dramatically improve forecast accuracy. Logility's website claims that "in benchmark tests, Voyager Demand Planning has improved accuracy as much as 80% over other forecasting methods."[16]

There are essentially two approaches to trying to determine what a reasonable forecast accuracy target is for a given set of products. The first is benchmarking, in which you look at competitors to understand how well they forecast. This does not provide a very satisfactory answer, though, because competitors generally have different products serving different market segments or regions and, more to the point, may not be forecasting well either. The second, which is the approach I recommend, is to analyze historical sales to understand the underlying variability of demand. By estimating demand variability that cannot be explained from known causes, you can estimate what forecast accuracy is theoretically achievable.

The assumption underlying this analytical approach is that the variability in demand across a selected segment of SKUs, once the baseline, trend, and seasonality factors affecting the demand are removed, is due to stationary noise from an unknown probability distribution. The idea is to estimate this unknown probability distribution (or at least the mean and standard deviation). The distribution in turn is then used to estimate theoretical achievable forecast accuracy by assuming that we are capable of accurately forecasting the mean of the demand, which is the best we can hope to do in practice. Though the methodology is far from perfect, it will give at least some idea of what can reasonably be achieved, which is certainly better than no information at all.

While alternative algorithms are possible, one approach consists of the following steps, which should be applied to a segment of SKUs that you have reason to believe follow similar demand patterns and that are affected by the same underlying demand variability. The steps are similar to the approach outlined earlier for determining seasonality indices. We assume that we have at least 1 year of historical sales data available for the SKUs that compose the segment that we are analyzing.

1. Divide the data into individual complete 1-year observation sets. This means that if sales data exists for an SKU for 2.5 years, take 2 complete calendar years of data (discarding the remaining data), and break these 2 years into two 1-year sets, with the first element of each series corresponding to the first month (January) of the calendar year.

2. Normalize each 1-year observation set by dividing each value by the mean of the observation set.

3. Perform a linear regression across all observations using time (as trend) and dummy variables for each month (excluding one) as the independent variables.

4. Use the resulting regression model to remove the "explained" variance from the observation sets, resulting in a set of normalized, stationary observations of demand.

5. Calculate the sample mean and standard deviation of the observations and divide the standard deviation by the mean to obtain an estimate of the coefficient of variation (CV).

6. Assume a distribution for demand or attempt to fit a distribution to the observations using a statistical test such as the chi-square test, the Kolmogorov–Smirnov test or the Anderson–Darling test. Based on this distribution, determine the forecast accuracy that is achievable given the mean and standard deviation calculated in step 5.

The final step of the algorithm may require the use of simulation to estimate the value of the forecast accuracy metric but is not difficult to perform using spreadsheet simulation tools.

Figure 2.11 shows the 1 – mMAPE forecast accuracy that is achievable as a function of the coefficient of variation of demand when the underlying demand follows a lognormal distribution. The values in Figure 2.11 were determined using a simulation of a lognormal distribution with a mean of 100 and a range of CVs varying from ~0 to 2. The output of each simulation was the estimate of the (1 – mMAPE) metric. Reading from this figure, if the CV is 0.5, achievable forecast accuracy is about 70%. This does not say that for any particular period you will observe a forecast accuracy no greater than 70%. Of course, you can get lucky, but what this is saying is that over a sufficiently large sample, your forecast accuracy can do no better than 70% if the underlying demand variability has a CV of ~0.53 and follows a lognormal distribution. If the CV is 1.0, the achievable forecast accuracy drops to about 55%. It's important to point out that the choice of distribution does matter. For example, a triangular distribution with a lower bound of 100, an upper bound of 1,225, and a most likely value of 200 has a CV of very close to 0.5 and yields an achievable forecast accuracy of only about 26%. This gives some sense of how important it is to try to understand the shape of the demand distribution—without this knowledge, calculating a reliable estimate of what forecast accuracy is achievable is difficult.

If you carry out this analysis, you may find that your actual forecast accuracy is close to the theoretical best you can achieve and may therefore decide that investing in improved forecasting is not your top priority. Most likely, however, you will discover that there is ample room for improvement, at least for some SKU segments.

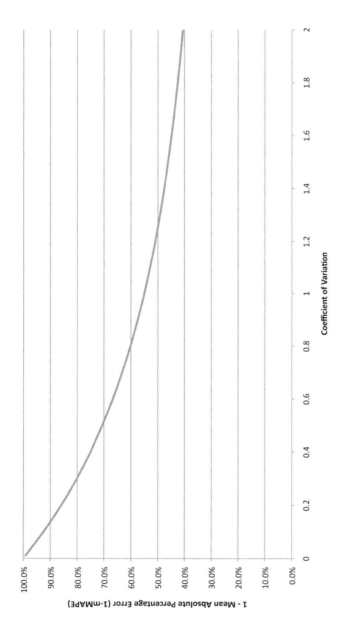

Figure 2.11. Achievable forecast accuracy as a function of demand variability (assuming lognormal distribution).

Making Management Reports Actionable

One of the key deficiencies in the way forecast accuracy is often reported to management is that little insight is provided about how to improve accuracy. The key is to understand the root causes of forecast error and to identify actions to address the root causes where possible. The key components of an actionable forecast accuracy report are the following:

- A summary, by SKU segment, of current forecast accuracy compared to both past forecast accuracy and estimated theoretically achievable forecast accuracy. This should include both an overall weighted average of forecast accuracy and histograms of forecast accuracy to understand the variation among the SKUs in the segment. Figure 2.12 shows a sample of what such a summary report might look like.
- A report showing how alternative statistical forecast methods performed on the SKU segments with subpar forecast accuracy.
- A summary, by SKU segment, of forecast bias, as illustrated in Figure 2.9, highlighting those items that have been significantly and consistently over- or underforecasted
- A report, by SKU segment, showing forecast accuracy over time alongside broader company metrics that should be affected by forecast accuracy—for example, customer service levels, inventory levels, and order expediting costs.

What actions should be taken on the basis of these reports?

- *Address problems with forecast bias first.* It is almost always the case in practice that systematic overforecasting or underforecasting is due to manual overrides to the forecast. In most cases, this behavior can be stopped by identifying those SKUs where the under- and overforecasting is occurring and preventing manual overrides from occurring in the future. In the unlikely event that the bias was caused either by chance or by other causes, the SKU can be examined to see if the statistical forecast method being applied is not the best or if it perhaps

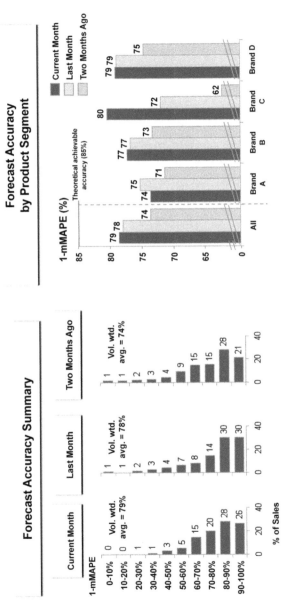

Figure 2.12. Sample forecast accuracy report.

does not belong in the class of stable products and therefore should not be forecasted using statistical methods.

- *Examine SKUs with high forecast error but no bias.* First, determine if the SKU belongs to the class of stable SKUs. If sales of the product are exhibiting signs of either end-of-life or introduction of a new product, the SKU should perhaps be moved into a different category and forecasted differently. If that is not the situation, examine the performance of alternative statistical forecasting methods to see if another method consistently outperforms this method. If so, consider switching to an alternative method. If not, it may be the case that the achievable forecast accuracy estimate for this SKU is overly optimistic. In this case, there is not much that can be done but to continue to monitor forecast performance for this SKU over time.

- *Examine transition product forecasts.* If the product has a high forecast error and the product is a transition product (either end-of-life or a new product), determine whether the transition profile was the root cause of the forecast error. If so, decide if another transition profile would have performed better and whether the transition profile should be changed for other products as well.

The Value of Improved Forecasting

What is it worth to improve forecast accuracy by, say, 15%? The benefits are usually tied to reduced inventory costs, reduced logistics costs associated with order expediting and transshipments, and improved service levels. By itself, an improvement in forecast accuracy will not magically result in cost savings. Actual savings will accrue only if concrete changes are made that result in lower safety stock, less order expediting, or fewer transshipments. If forecast accuracy improves but the purchasing system's safety stock parameter is still set to 5 weeks of supply, inventory levels will not come down. Also, if there is significant bias in the forecast, reducing the amount of overforecasting will result in a reduction in inventory levels, but reducing the amount of underforecasting may result in an increase in inventory levels.

It is obvious that tying forecast accuracy to specific cost reductions or service level improvements is critical to getting management buy-in that forecasting accuracy improvement is valuable. More often overlooked is that making these ties explicit is key to getting the improvements in the first place. Forecasters will take their work more seriously and drive to a better result if the cost savings from improved forecast accuracy are clearly reported. Unfortunately, in most companies, the connection between forecast accuracy and cost savings is only given lip service. Part of the reason is that it is difficult to attribute an improvement in service levels or a reduction in expediting costs solely to forecast improvements. But over time, you should observe a correlation between these metrics. If the correlation is tenuous or nonexistent, that may provide the impetus to figure out why the benefits to improved forecast accuracy are not being realized. At the very least, reporting service levels, safety stock levels, order expediting costs, and transshipment costs alongside forecast accuracy metrics will provide management with a way to observe the effects of forecast accuracy over time.

But what about estimating the value of improved forecast accuracy before you make any investment in forecast process improvement? Answering this question is often critical for getting budgets allocated to forecasting. There is one way in which an analytical framework can help to at least estimate the savings in inventory, through safety stock reduction, that an improvement in forecast accuracy can provide. Whether you achieve these savings in practice depends on whether you reduce your safety stock in response to improved service levels. The idea is to estimate the gap between the actual and theoretical forecast accuracy and how much reduction in safety stock would accrue by closing that gap. To perform the estimate, you need to have an estimate of what your current forecast accuracy is and what your achievable forecast accuracy is. Suppose, for example, that your current forecast accuracy (as measured by the mMAPE metric, for example) is 50%, and you estimate achievable forecast accuracy as 70%. If you maintain your customer service level, measured by fill rate, at 98%, how much of a reduction in safety stock can you expect by improving your forecast accuracy from 50% to the achievable level of 70%? The following procedure provides one way to estimate the answer to this question:

1. Estimate the effective change in the coefficient of variation that results in going from 50% forecast accuracy to 70%. Assuming that demand follows a lognormal distribution, we can read from Figure 2.11 that a 50% forecast accuracy corresponds to a CV of ~1.2, and 70% forecast accuracy corresponds to a CV of ~0.5.
2. Calculate the quantity of on-hand inventory required to achieve a 98% fill rate when demand per period follows a lognormal distribution with a CV of 0.5 versus a CV of 1.2.
3. Estimate the percent reduction in on-hand inventory that would result by reducing the CV of demand from 1.2 to 0.5.

This procedure can be refined in a number of ways, but it provides a rough estimate of the kinds of benefits that can be achieved. In this example, the reduction in on-hand inventory comes to approximately 39%. If we believed that a more reasonable goal would not be to achieve 70% accuracy but only 60%, the percent reduction in on-hand inventory would be approximately 23%. This kind of rough analysis is useful to estimate potential benefits in inventory reductions resulting from improved forecast accuracy but should be used with caution: Actual benefits will vary.

Investing in Improved Forecasting

At this point, you may be convinced that an investment to improve your forecasting process is worthwhile. What is the best way to invest in such improvements? The common answer is to get a better software system. While this may be part of the answer, it is not the whole answer. Investing in a new software system should only come after careful thought about what such a system needs to be able to do. That means figuring out in detail how your forecasting process needs to change, what additional reports need to be generated, what new inputs are needed, and what functions can reasonably be automated through software.

One approach that has been successful is to construct a pilot process using inexpensive, readily available software to work out the details of a new process and test its effectiveness. The prototype functionality and reports created as part of the pilot can then serve as detailed requirements when rolling out the process more broadly.

In most cases, companies already have some software in place that performs some forecasting functions. The challenge then is to determine whether to modify the existing system, supplement its functionality with another system, or replace the current system with a new system. By performing a pilot and then comparing the requirements from the pilot with the capabilities of the existing system, you can often start to build a consensus about the most sensible path to improving the forecast system and process.

CHAPTER 3

Sales and Operations Planning

Plans are nothing; planning is everything.

—Dwight D. Eisenhower

The origins of the term "sales and operations planning" are unclear, but the process was first written about explicitly in a book by Richard C. Ling and Walter E. Goddard titled *Orchestrating Success: Improve Control of the Business with Sales and Operations Planning* and published in 1988. The authors acknowledge the importance of Oliver Wight, one of the pioneers of MRP II (manufacturing resource planning) systems, in shaping their thinking about the process. Indeed, MRP (material requirements planning) and MRP II were both important precursors to the development of the sales and operations planning (S&OP) process. In their book, Ling and Goddard describe the S&OP process as orchestrating the activities of different departments within an organization so that they are working toward a consistent plan:

> Any good general manager can harmonize his company through a process called "sales and operations planning," in which he meets with his top managers on a regular and frequent basis to update the plans for all departments. The plans take into account projections made by the sales and marketing departments, the resources available from manufacturing, engineering, purchasing, and finance, and are directed toward hitting the company's objectives. Sales and operations planning is done on an aggregate or family level, and covers a sufficient span of time to make sure that the necessary resources will be available. The approved aggregate plans drive the individual departmental detail plans. Each month—or more frequently if the market conditions are volatile—their representatives

meet again to determine whether the overall company plan is on course, and to adjust for changes in the marketplace and changes or problems within the company.[1]

Several books on the S&OP process have since appeared that provide both case studies on how S&OP processes work within specific companies and advice on how to implement an effective S&OP process.[2] The common theme emphasized in these books is the importance of having all functions within a company working toward a realistic sales and operations plan, one that all parties understand and agree is achievable. In the absence of such a plan, and a way to ensure that the operating plans of each department are working toward this plan, the business typically suffers with poor customer service, excess inventory, low profit margins, and a repeating cycle of expedited orders, premium freight, and disappointed customers and suppliers.

While the S&OP process has been around for a relatively short time compared to forecasting, the principal question that the S&OP process addresses has been wrestled with for a long time: Given an unbiased forecast, what should a company position itself to acquire, build, and sell? The answer to this question is variously referred to as a *sales and operations plan*, a *business plan*, or a *supply plan*. It is the most critical output of the S&OP process and serves to guide the direction of all functions within a company. A sales and operations plan depends on supply availability, manufacturing and distribution resource constraints, and demand uncertainty. In the absence of any of these factors, there would be little reason to deviate from the unbiased forecast. If you know for certain what your demand for products is going to be, you have no problem obtaining enough raw materials to produce the products, you have the manufacturing capacity to produce the products on time, and you have the distribution capacity to deliver the products to customers, then planning and executing to the unbiased forecast is straightforward.

When constraints arise and when demand is uncertain, the question is more difficult to answer and the chances for miscommunication and lack of coordination within the company and across the supply chain increase. For example, suppose a company produces and sells two products, both of which utilize the same part whose supply unexpectedly becomes constrained. In a company that lacks an effective S&OP process, events might unfold like this: The constraint on the part would likely become apparent first to procurement in the form of a phone call from the supplier, a lead time extension, or a delivery that is short of the purchase order quantity. Procurement would then communicate the shortage to manufacturing, who would then decide how much of each product to produce so as not to exceed the available supply. When this decision is made, sales may not be forewarned so they continue to sell as though no supply constraint exists, perhaps booking sales of products in excess of available supply, thereby ensuring some customers will not receive their orders on time. In a company with an S&OP process in place, when procurement is notified of a supply constraint, representatives from sales, marketing, finance, manufacturing, and procurement, as well as the general manager for the business, would convene to decide how to alter production and sales plans to address the shortage. The decision, jointly arrived at, would then drive activities in each department to respond to the shortage. For example, procurement might need to cancel or delay outstanding purchase orders (POs) on other parts that might not be needed, manufacturing might need to alter its production plans, and sales might need to undertake demand conditioning activities to steer customers to available supply.

But the S&OP process is not just about coordinating and synchronizing responses to unforeseen events, such as supply shortages, across different functions of an organization. It is also about anticipating future outcomes in such a way that the company is best positioned to profit from uncertain future events. This means using the knowledge about future demand and supply—incomplete and uncertain as it is—to make the best possible decisions about what to procure, produce, and sell. In a nutshell, the role of the S&OP process is to take the unconstrained demand forecast and decide—based on an understanding of demand variability, supply constraints, market objectives, and competitive assessments—what is the right service level to target for each product and what is the right level of supply required to meet that service level. Setting these targets—both for levels of supply and service levels—and measuring progress toward achieving them are the key functions of the S&OP process.

The S&OP process needs to be tailored to the specific constraints that each company has to contend with. In this chapter, I discuss the many practical challenges that arise in implementing an S&OP process and suggest useful ways of dealing with them. My approach is to start with the simplest possible setting for an S&OP process—one in which there is only one product for sale and the only consideration is demand uncertainty. This "newsvendor problem," as it is usually referred to, serves as a useful starting point to understand one of the basic trade-offs in S&OP. I then introduce additional complexities one at a time, discussing approaches to dealing with each. By proceeding in this incremental fashion, I want to make it apparent how both the basic paradigm of the S&OP process exists even in the extremely simple setting of the newsvendor problem and how the S&OP process can be tailored to different environments, depending on the degree of complexity present and on what constraints are operative.

A Note on Aggregate Planning

Some operations management texts, while they do not discuss the S&OP process, do cover aggregate planning. Aggregate planning usually refers to the activities associated with ensuring adequate production and distribution capacity is in place to meet future demand. As implied by its name, aggregate planning is typically undertaken at a brand level by month or quarter because questions of capacity can often be addressed at this level of granularity without loss of fidelity. Aggregate planning, however, is not the same as S&OP. The key difference is that aggregate planning does not purport to wrestle with the problem of what fraction of unknown future demand to plan for while this is the central problem addressed by the S&OP process. Aggregate planning assumes that demand is given; S&OP decides what demand to plan for given demand uncertainty and supply constraints. In this sense, one can view aggregate planning as a complementary planning activity that occurs to address capacity issues once the S&OP process has determined the sales and operations plan. Some of the issues related to aggregate planning are discussed in chapter 4 in the section titled "Strategic Issues in Inventory and Supply Planning."

The S&OP Process in Simplest Form: The Newsvendor Problem

In most introductory inventory management textbooks, the newsvendor (or newsboy) problem is the canonical example used to illustrate the trade-off between holding too little inventory and thereby missing potential sales and holding too much inventory and thereby having left-over, unsold inventory.[3] The solution to the problem shows that there is an optimal quantity of inventory to acquire to maximize expected profit in the face of uncertain demand. What is not emphasized in these text-books, however, is that the newsvendor problem also serves as a starting point for understanding why the S&OP process is fundamental to the decision process of how much product should be acquired, produced, and sold when future demand is uncertain. In fact, the newsvendor prob-lem illustrates in an extremely simple form what the S&OP process is intended to accomplish. It is therefore an ideal starting point for under-standing the process.

In its usual formulation, a newsvendor must decide how many news-papers to procure at the beginning of the day prior to observing what the demand for papers will be. He purchases the papers at a cost of $c each and he sells each paper for $p. At the end of the day, unsold papers can be sold for a salvage value of $s each. Although the newsvendor does not know the exact demand for papers, he does know the cumulative probability distribution of demand, $F(x)$. That is, he knows not only the unbiased forecast of demand (the expected value of the demand distribu-tion) but also the *entire* distribution of demand. The problem for the newsvendor is to compute the number of papers he should buy at the start of the day to maximize his *expected* profit. If D is a random variable representing the demand for papers, which has the probability distribu-tion $F(x)$, and q is the quantity of papers he purchases at the start of the day, his profit will be

$$\text{Profit} = p \min(D,q) + s \max(q - D,0) - qc.$$

The problem is to figure out what value of q maximizes the *expected value* of the profit. The optimal value of q in this case turns out to be

$$q^* = F^{-1}\left(\frac{p-c}{p-s} \right).$$

While this solution can be derived easily enough using calculus, a more insightful approach to understanding the solution is to consider the mar-ginal profit of procuring an additional newspaper. For every additional newspaper that is procured, there is a decreasing probability that it will be sold. At a certain point, the probability of an additional sale multiplied by the profit received from that sale does not exceed the probability that there won't be an additional sale multiplied by the loss from the unsold unit. This is precisely the point at which it does not pay to procure any additional papers. The marginal expected profit from selling an additional paper beyond q papers is

$$MP(q) = (p - c)P(D > q) - (c - s)P(D \leq q).$$

When this marginal expected profit function becomes negative, it no longer pays to procure additional papers. This occurs at the value of q for which $MP(q) = 0$. Recognizing that $P(D > q) = 1 - P(D \leq q)$ and that $P(D \leq q) = F(q)$, you can solve $MP(q) = 0$ for q and obtain the solution q^* above.

If you think of the quantity $(p - c) / p$ as the contribution margin for newspapers and for the moment assume the salvage value is zero, you can interpret the previous solution as saying that the newsvendor should procure enough newspapers such that the probability that a stock-out does not occur equals the contribution margin. So only if the contribution margin is 50% or greater (when the salvage value is 0) would the solution recommend procuring more than the median value of demand. Given that a 50% margin for most businesses is quite high, this result may seem surprising. But it only makes sense if the items in question are extremely perishable, such as newspapers, and the salvage value is low. Most functional consumer packaged goods or groceries have low contribution margins but also have relatively long shelf lives. The salvage value is effectively high in this case because there will be future opportunities to sell the leftover items. Newspapers have modest contribution margins at the retail level but are highly perishable. This means that it might make sense for the newspaper supplier to artificially supplement the salvage value to encourage newsvendors to stock enough newspapers to meet a high fraction of demand. In fact, many publishers offer full value back to the retailers on unsold newspapers, which effectively means the retailer has an incentive to provide a 100% service level.

In the newsvendor problem, any order quantity q that is selected has an associated service level. The service level can be measured in two ways: as a stock-out probability—that is, the probability that the demand outstrips the supply for newspapers during the day and as a fill rate, the expected fraction of demand that is met. For a given procurement quantity q, the stock-out probability is defined as

$$\text{stock-out probability} \equiv P(D > q) = 1 - F(q).$$

The fill rate is defined as

$$\text{Fill rate} \equiv \frac{E\left[\min(D,q)\right]}{E[X]} = \frac{\int_0^q x dF(x) + q\left[1 - F(q)\right]}{\int_0^\infty x dF(x)}$$

The solution to the newsvendor problem results in an implied optimal stock-out probability and fill rate. By the same token, if you simply wanted to achieve some target service level, you could use either of these equations to solve for the corresponding order quantity that would achieve the target. In this way, you can easily see the fundamental trade-off between inventory investment and customer service levels that exists in all supply chains. In this simple case, this trade-off can be captured in exact analytical form. In more complex scenarios, the trade-off can only be quantified approximately.

Figure 3.1 illustrates the optimal order quantity in the newsvendor problem when $p = \$1.00$, $c = \$0.60$, $s = \$0.56$, and the distribution of

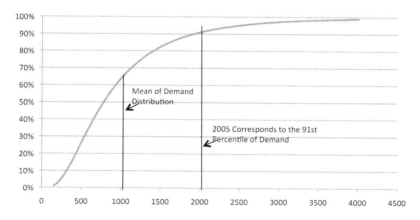

Figure 3.1. Solution to newsvendor problem. Demand is lognormal with a mean of 1,000 and standard deviation of 800. The solution that optimizes expected profit covers 91% of the demand distribution.

demand is lognormal with a mean of 1,000 and standard deviation of 800. Then $(p - c) / (p - s) \sim 0.91$. In this instance, the newsvendor would purchase approximately 2,005 newspapers to maximize his expected profits. If the newsvendor were to purchase 2,005 papers, his expected profit would be ~$324 and the fill rate (the percent of demand that is filled) would be ~98%. On the other hand, if he were to purchase the forecasted demand (i.e., the mean demand) of 1,000, his expected profit would only be $279 and the fill rate would be ~88%.

Figure 3.2 shows the marginal profit and achieved fill rate for different supply quantities for the newsvendor problem. This view can be useful in helping to decide the appropriate level of supply to plan for in the S&OP process.

The critical point to observe from this analysis is that by deliberately purchasing more than twice the forecasted demand, the newsvendor improves his expected profitability by about 16%. In doing so, he has decided to target a higher service level (measured as fill rate) of 98% rather than the 88% that he would have achieved by planning for the forecasted demand. From a supply chain planning perspective, this result is key to understanding why an S&OP process is necessary: The output of the forecasting process—the unbiased forecast—only tells you what the expected future demand will be, not the quantity you should plan to supply. If demand were known precisely, this would be the end of the story: You would simply procure the unconstrained forecast quantity,

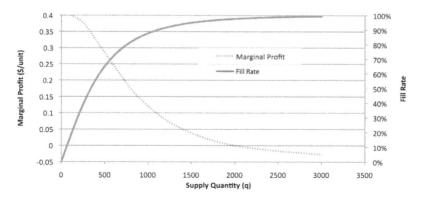

Figure 3.2. Marginal profit function and fill rate as function of supply quantity for newsvendor problem.

which would result in a 100% service level and zero remaining inventory. But as soon as demand becomes uncertain, the optimal decision becomes more complex and depends on knowledge of the demand distribution, not just the mean unconstrained forecast. That is why estimating the demand distribution—either by making use of forecast error measurements to estimate demand variability or by explicitly creating an unconstrained forecast that includes a range of values—is so critical to an effective S&OP process.

It's worth pausing to emphasize what the inputs and outputs of the S&OP process are in this simple setting. The inputs are the price, cost, salvage value of the newspaper, and the distribution of demand. The outputs are the procurement quantity (i.e., the quantity of newspapers to buy), the expected service level, the expected profit, and the expected quantity of newspapers sold and salvaged. In the more complex setting of a real business, there are more inputs to the process (including statements about supply constraints) and more outputs, but these inputs and outputs, in various guises, remain the predominant ones.

The process itself (which takes the inputs and generates the outputs) is, in the setting of the newsvendor problem, almost trivial because the solution can be generated through the application of an analytical formula. However, in a more realistic setting, there is no such analytical formula and the process requires far more deliberation and judgment to carry out.

Deficiencies of the Newsvendor Problem

The newsvendor problem has a number deficiencies and unrealistic assumptions that make it difficult to generalize and apply in practice:

- The impact on future demand due to poor service levels is not captured. That is, the model assumes that there is no cost of lost sales beyond the loss of revenue from demand not met in the current period. Most companies place a premium on achieving high service levels because customers who find that a product is not available or is delayed are more likely not to return in the future.

- There are no capacity or supply constraints. The newsvendor is able to order any number of papers he wants. In reality, companies must deal with a variety of capacity and supply constraints.
  - Manufacturing production capacity limits
  - Minimum order quantities
  - Constraints on transportation lane capacity and container size restrictions
  - Working capital restrictions
  - Raw material shortages

- There is only a single product. Companies at any given time may sell thousands of different products at different points in their life cycles. The interaction effects of these different products on overall company performance are complex. Optimizing the expected profit of each product (in each market region or customer segment) in isolation from all other products the companies sells will not lead to an overall optimal or even feasible solution for the company.
- The distribution of demand is assumed known. In practice, a company may, at best, have at its disposal an unbiased forecast of demand and some measure of forecast accuracy that enables some estimate of the range of demand but certainly nothing highly precise regarding the shape of the demand distribution.
- The only objective considered is maximizing expected profit. In reality, companies have varied objectives. For example, capturing market share for some products may be deemed more important than maximizing profitability, at least in the short term.

The existence of all these issues is what makes the S&OP process in practice far more complex to execute than solving the newsvendor problem. It should be clear that even if you could agree on a single objective to optimize and you further assumed that all the data required as input were readily available, the resulting problem would be so complex as to be analytically intractable.[4] The fact that there are multiple competing objectives and that the data available is likely to be both incomplete and inaccurate only adds to the difficulties of finding a solution. For these reasons, the S&OP process, while it can benefit from the application of analytical tools, is ultimately a process requiring the informed judgment of individuals who have a stake in the outcome. There is no single right answer for the S&OP process, but the practical challenge for any company is finding a good solution to this problem—one that comes close to maximizing expected profit over a reasonable horizon but that is also feasible and considers other objectives in a balanced way—and doing so on a repeatable basis as markets evolve and products change.

Addressing Demand Variability

As the newsvendor problem demonstrates, knowledge of demand variability—ideally, knowledge of the entire demand distribution—is critical to making good S&OP decisions. Without it, you cannot estimate the marginal value of procuring and holding additional supply. And yet little attention is usually given to understanding demand variability. When asked how they measure demand variability, most supply chain directors say they measure forecast error. But forecast error is not the same as demand variability. The distinction is not just theoretical. Forecast error says just as much about your ability to forecast as it does about the inherent variability of demand. Demand variability is the true fluctuation in demand unadulterated by poor (or even good) forecasting.

Just a few years ago, there were enormous practical challenges associated with collecting and storing large amounts of data on past sales and forecasts, as well as enabling the use of analytical tools to understand the data. As a result, little effort was expended to try to estimate any characteristics of demand based on historical sales or forecasts, beyond simply generating an unbiased forecast. Today, enormous quantities of data on past sales and forecasts are routinely stored in data warehouses where they can be easily mined using powerful analytical software. The result is that there is little excuse not to turn the full power of statistical analysis on the problem of understanding and characterizing the nature of demand. An important step in this direction is trying to understand demand variability and using this information to make better informed decisions in the S&OP process.

In discussing demand variability, it's helpful to make a distinction between two sources of variability that drive forecast error: inherent demand variability and error introduced due to (imperfect) forecasting. A reasonable model to characterize these two sources of variability is to represent the forecast as the sum of the underlying demand signal plus a forecast error signal:

$$F(t,t + n) = X(t + n) + \varepsilon(t,t + n).$$

What this says is that the forecast for period $t + n$ standing at the beginning of period t is the sum of the unknown demand in period $t + n$ plus an error term that is the forecast signal error. In this model, the best forecast you can obtain is the expected value of $F(t,t + n)$; what you actually obtain in forecasting is a single sample (or perhaps multiple samples) from the distribution of $F(t,t + n)$. Only if the expected value of $\varepsilon(t,t + n) = 0$ is the forecast unbiased. Also, in most cases, the variance of the term $\varepsilon(t,t + n)$ will increase with n, meaning that the forecast error signal degrades the further out you are forecasting. Thinking of the forecast process in this way is helpful because it provides a framework for understanding to what extent forecast error is driven by the underlying demand variability ($X(t + n)$) or by the forecast signal error ($\varepsilon(t,t + n)$). In this context, a perfect forecast would be one in which $\varepsilon(t,t + n) = 0$, but this would not mean that your forecast error would be zero: There would still be noise in the signal due to the inherent variability in demand.

Understanding Demand Variability: Standard Deviation Versus Distribution

Understanding demand variability and incorporating information about it—imperfect as it may be—into the S&OP process is critical. But capturing reliable information about demand variability is a challenge. One key decision is how to go about estimating demand variability. Another is how to report demand variability to management and S&OP participants who are likely not versed in statistical and probabilistic concepts.

A basic measure of demand variability is standard deviation. Obtaining an estimate of standard deviation of demand should be an ongoing function of the S&OP process. But while the standard deviation is an important measure of variability, it is by no means enough to capture all aspects of variability. One point often lost among those not trained in probability and statistics is that variability of demand is only partly explained via standard deviation.

For example, consider an item whose unbiased forecast is for 1,000 units, and suppose the standard deviation of demand has been estimated at 800. If you assume the demand is normally distributed with this mean and standard deviation, to cover 98% of the demand distribution, you would need to plan for 2,643 units. On the other hand, if you assume demand follows a gamma distribution *with this same mean and standard deviation*, you would need to plan for 3,224 units, an increase of 22% over the normal distribution. If you assume demand follows a lognormal distribution, you would need to plan for 3,311 units, an increase of 25% over the amount required for the normal distribution. In other words, even if the mean and standard deviation of demand remain the same, the quantity of supply required to meet a given percentage of demand may change dramatically depending on the shape of the demand distribution that is assumed and what percent of the demand distribution is covered.

The normal distribution generally gives rise to a conservative estimate of what is required to cover a given fraction of demand with a specified mean and standard deviation because the tail of a normal distribution tapers off relatively quickly. And yet, the normal distribution is perhaps the most widely used for representing demand. The assumption of normally distributed demand is embedded in the logic of many supply chain software systems. And yet little empirical evidence exists to support the hypothesis that demand in any industry or for any company follows a normal distribution. In fact, most sales data show spikes in demand, even after explanatory effects due to promotions and other factors are removed, which would not be predicted if the demand distribution were normal. By assuming demand is normally distributed, you are likely underestimating the chances of large deviations in demand and may have unrealistic expectations about how well you are therefore positioned to respond to demand.

Because demand variability is affected by the shape of the demand distribution—and not just through either the standard deviation of demand or specific quantiles of the demand distribution—it is worthwhile to undertake from time to time an analysis to better understand the actual shape of the demand distribution. This can be done by performing formal statistical tests such as the chi-square test, the

Kolmogorov–Smirnov test and the Anderson–Darling test, on past sales data. Alternatively, constructing and analyzing empirical distributions based on past sales history can illuminate demand patterns and tendencies. One of the most useful outcomes of such analyses is gaining a better understanding of the tail of demand distributions—that is, what the likelihood is of large demand spikes. This understanding directly affects the S&OP process because one of the key decisions is deciding how much higher the plan should be beyond the unbiased forecast. If the tail of the demand distribution is heavy—meaning the likelihood of demand spikes occurring is much larger than what would be predicted by, for example, assuming that demand is normally distributed—then that might lead the S&OP process in certain cases to elect to plan for significantly more than the unbiased forecast in order to capture the potential upside in demand.

Estimating Demand Standard Deviation

Estimating the standard deviation of demand is an activity that should be undertaken as a regular part of the S&OP process. There are numerous approaches that can be used, three of which are outlined below. The right approach may not be the same for all stock-keeping units (SKUs) and may change over time. Each will almost certainly give different results. There is little research to draw on to help you decide which approach is most suitable. It may be worthwhile to try more than one approach. If they give very different results, you can use this fact as a basis for further investigation.

As a practical matter, it is sometimes easier to estimate the coefficient of variation (CV) of demand, defined as the standard deviation divided by the mean (unbiased forecast). To obtain an estimate of the standard deviation of demand in any period, simply multiply the CV by the unbiased forecast or mean demand. Because the CV is scale invariant, it can be used to characterize demand variability regardless of what the mean demand is. Given the mean demand, specifying the CV is equivalent to specifying the standard deviation.

Use Historical Sales Data

An algorithm similar to steps 1–5 of the procedure described in chapter 2 in the section titled "What Is Achievable? Placing Forecast Accuracy in Context" can be utilized to estimate the coefficient of variation of demand for an SKU or a group of SKUs. The following are some caveats:

- It's important to make an effort to remove all sources of explained variance from the sales data including seasonality, trend, and promotions. Different methods can be used to do this. In step 3, performing a regression is the proposed approach to remove seasonality from the data. Alternatively, you can use the forecasting seasonality profiles to remove seasonality. Removing promotions may need to be done manually, at least at first, until a reliable way of automating the removal of promotion effects can be determined.

- If regression is used to remove explained variance due to seasonality from the data, it should be applied to a reasonably large set of data (for example, at least 50 sets of observations) or the variance explained by the dummy variables may be exaggerated.

- Apparent outliers that remain in the data after the regression has been performed, and after the variability due to the explanatory variables has been removed, should be kept in the data. The purpose of the analysis is to understand true demand variability, which often has unexplained spikes and troughs. This is the nature of a random process.

Use Forecast Error Metrics

If the forecast process outputs a forecast error metric, such as any of the metrics described in chapter 2, this information can be used as the basis for estimating the standard deviation of demand. Procedures for transforming the forecast error metric into an estimate of standard deviation of demand are not well documented. One commonly recommended approach is to multiply the mean absolute deviation (MAD) metric by 1.25.[5] The justification for this calculation is based on an assumption that demand follows a normal distribution. A more general approach, which can be used for any metric and any assumed underlying demand distribution, is the following:

1. Obtain an average forecast error metric for an SKU or group of SKUs. This may require some processing of the forecast error metric reported by the forecasting function either to obtain an average across a set of SKUs or to decide what forecast horizon to utilize.

2. If the forecast error metric is not scale invariant (e.g., MAD, mean squared error [MSE]), then obtain an estimate of the mean demand corresponding to forecast error in step 1. If the metric is scale invariant (e.g., mean absolute percentage error [MAPE], modified mean absolute percentage error mMAPE), pick a value to serve as the mean demand (e.g., 100).

3. Assume an underlying demand distribution—say, a lognormal distribution.

4. Compute a standard deviation that gives rise to the average forecast error determined in step 1. This can most easily be accomplished via a spreadsheet simulation. The coefficient of variation estimate is the standard deviation divided by the mean.

5. Calculate the standard deviation of demand for any SKU in any period by multiplying the CV by the unbiased forecast.

To illustrate the approach, consider a product that has an mMAPE forecast error of 30%. If you assume a lognormal distribution for demand, you can utilize Figure 2.11 to determine the CV of demand given a forecast accuracy (1 – mMAPE) value of 70%, which yields a CV of approximately 0.53.

The forecast error metric will reflect both systematic errors in forecasting and inherent demand variability. In the previous example, the CV estimate of 0.53 includes both variability due to demand and forecast signal error. This gives rise to the question of whether it is important to try to separate out the variability due to forecast error and variability due to inherent demand uncertainty. Because there is no obvious way to do this, the usual assumption is to treat all the variability as coming from inherent demand variability, which amounts to assuming that the forecast perfectly estimates the mean of the demand distribution. Such an assumption is optimistic to say the least. Some argue that the distinction between forecast error and demand variability is not important: What's important is the overall variability that results from the noisy demand signal filtered through an imperfect forecasting signal. Following this line of thought, the estimate of demand variability should include additional error introduced because of imperfect forecasting. For the purposes of safety stock planning, this makes sense—you need to protect against both demand variability and forecast error. The problem with lumping the two sources of variability together is that it becomes impossible to estimate how much reduction in error can be achieved through improved forecasting.

One benefit of this approach compared to the first approach is that it has the potential to help understand how the forecast signal degrades as you look further out over time. For example, forecast accuracy 1 month ahead usually is better than it is 2 months ahead. This does not mean that demand variability increases as you look further ahead but simply that the forecast error increases as you forecast further out. By looking at the CV of demand based on forecast accuracy metrics at 1, 2, and 3 months ahead, for example, you can get a sense of how much forecast signal degradation occurs as you look further ahead in time. In fact, such an analysis could in principle help to separate out the causes of forecast error into inherent demand signal variability and forecast signal error.

Use Forecast Bounds

In some instances, the forecast process may output an explicit range of values for each forecasted product. That is, in addition to forecasting the expected demand in future periods, the forecast process will generate an upper and lower bound on the demand. In this case, these bounds can be utilized to obtain an estimate of the standard deviation of demand. The bounds usually correspond to some quantiles of the demand distribution—for example, the 75th and 25th percentiles of the distribution. Turning these quantiles into an estimate of the standard deviation requires an assumption about the underlying demand distribution. The procedure consists of finding the parameters of the distribution that will result in a distribution with the desired mean and quantiles. The approach is straightforward but in most cases will require some numerical computation.

For example, suppose the forecast process indicates that the expected demand for a product is 100 with a 90th percentile of demand at 150 and a 10th percentile of demand at 50. This can be fit to a normal distribution with mean = 100 and standard deviation = 39.

Note, however, that it would be impossible to fit this same data to the lognormal distribution because the distribution is asymmetric and has only two parameters. If you drop the 10th percentile constraint, you can fit the mean and 90th percentile to a lognormal distribution with mean = 100 and standard deviation = 1,104. In this case, the 10th percentile of the fitted distribution = 0.5.

Incorporating Demand Variability Information Into the S&OP Process

Once a quantitative estimate of demand variability has been obtained, it is important for this information to be incorporated into the S&OP decision-making process. If, as is often the case, S&OP participants are accustomed to arguing their opinions in the absence of data about demand variability, the addition of this information will require a significant shift in thinking. Rather than basing decisions about how much to increase the sales and operations plan from the unbiased forecast on gut feel or on arbitrary revenue targets, the decision makers can now make use of explicit demand variability information to decide how much of the demand distribution to cover and what the resulting service level targets should be.

One of the concrete ways in which the S&OP process can incorporate demand variability information is by creating a graphical representation of the forecasts with demand distribution curves or quantile bands overlaid. In addition, initial recommendations on what percentage of the distribution to plan for based on profitability of the product or other considerations can be indicated on the charts as a way to provide a starting point for the S&OP discussions about where to position supply. Figure 3.3 provides an example of what such a graphical representation looks like.

In addition to providing information about the demand distribution, accountability should be enforced by reporting past performance: How much of the demand distribution was planned for coverage in the previous S&OP cycle, how much of this demand was realized, what were the achieved service levels, how much cost was incurred expediting to meet demand beyond the plan, and how much inventory cost (in the form of inventory holding costs, and reserves or write-offs against obsolete and surplus inventory) was incurred due to demand not being realized against the plan?

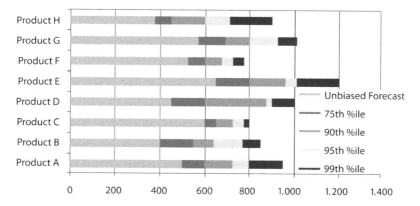

Figure 3.3. Sample presentation of demand distribution information in S&OP process. The different shades represent different percentiles of the forecast demand distribution over a 2-month horizon.

In reporting information on service levels, you should report on service levels for demand that came in below the planned coverage level separately from service levels for demand above the planned coverage level. For example, if you planned for the sale of 2,000 units but demand came in for 2,500, you should report the service levels on the first 2,000 separately from the 500 additional units. If the service level for the initial 2,000 was below target, you should undertake a root cause analysis to understand the reason for the shortfall. For the additional 500, for which you did not explicitly plan, the service level may have suffered or significant expedite expense may have been incurred to meet the additional demand. Reporting the costs of overachieving and underachieving the sales and operations plan clearly and prominently is an important mechanism to ensure thoughtful consideration of these trade-offs in future planning cycles.

Coping With Revenue Targets

The S&OP process is sometimes viewed as just a forecast fine-tuning exercise. The idea is that while the forecasting process is designed to create an unbiased forecast, the S&OP process is intended to adjust this forecast to align it with the strategic revenue targets for the company. In practice, this amounts to scaling the unbiased forecasts up to meet the revenue targets. In many companies, all the S&OP process really amounts to is ensuring that the forecast sums to the revenue targets. If it does not, the forecast needs to be modified so that it aligns with the targets. Often, this is done regardless of supply constraints, meaning that the scaling up of the unbiased forecast is done regardless of the ability to acquire, produce, and deliver the products. The thinking is that the supply and resource constraints can be solved later through, for example, chasing of parts, hiring temporary workers, or paying premium freight to expedite goods.

You can usually tell fairly easily if an S&OP process at a company is really just an exercise in scaling up the forecast to meet revenue targets: Talk to someone involved in the day-to-day process. At a major health care product supplier, the individual responsible for demand planning told me,

> After we finish generating the forecast, we roll up the numbers across the division and see if they add up to the targets that the division manager has set. They're almost always too low so we increase the forecasts to get a plan that matches the targets.[6]

There are three significant problems with this approach. First, it treats the revenue targets as a fixed constraint rather than what it really is: a goal, often overly aggressive, which may be appropriately modified or refined during the process. Second, the method of scaling the forecasts is typically done in an ad hoc fashion, most often uniformly across all products, not based on profitability of the products, the distribution of demand, nor available supply. And third, the costs of procuring and producing the goods needed to meet the revenue targets—in particular, the costs associated with expediting—are not explicitly incorporated into the decision-making process.

To understand why scaling up the unbiased forecast to meet the revenue objectives may not lead to a desirable plan, consider a slight variant of the newsvendor problem in which there are three products instead of one. Table 3.1 shows the cost, price, salvage value, unbiased forecast, and coefficient of variation of demand for each product. Suppose the target revenue from the sale of all products is $18,000. Producing to the unbiased forecast would result in a planned revenue of $12,900,[7] which

Table 3.1. Parameters for 3-Product Version of the Newsvendor Problem

	Cost ($/unit)	Price ($/unit)	Salvage value ($/unit)	Unbiased forecast (units)	CV of demand
Product A	6	11	5.9	500	0.8
Product B	4	6	2	700	0.6
Product C	3	4	2.75	800	0.4

would lead to an expected profit of $3,235 and service levels, reported as fill rates, of 88% for product A, 88% for product B, and 90% for product C, as shown in the upper left quadrant of Table 3.2.

If you impose the constraint that the sales and operations plan must have a planned revenue of $18,000, you must decide how to modify the forecasts so that the planned revenue equals the target revenue. In the usual approach, the unbiased forecast would be uniformly scaled up in such a way that the total planned revenue is $18,000. The upper right quadrant of Table 3.2 (labeled as "Linearly scaled forecast") shows the sales and operations plan using this approach. Following this plan leads to an expected profit of $3,274, not appreciably greater than planning for the unbiased forecast.

If, instead of scaling the forecasts uniformly, you scaled by marginal expected profit (by adding a unit of supply incrementally to the product that has the largest marginal expected profit until the revenue plan is achieved), you would realize an expected profit of $3,705, a 13% increase over the uniform scaling approach, as shown in the lower left quadrant of Table 3.2. In this case, the resulting service levels would be 98% for product A, 80% for product B, and 90% for product C.

For comparison purposes, the unconstrained solution, obtained by solving the newsvendor problem independently for each product, is displayed in the lower right quadrant of Table 3.2. The expected profit of this plan is $3,815, 3% higher than the expected profit of the marginal allocation plan with the $18,000 revenue target. The planned revenue in this case is around $26,000, primarily because of the large amount of sales targeted for product A. The unconstrained plan is targeting a near 100% service level for product A and to do this requires positioning supply at the far end of the demand distribution. In practice, such a plan

Table 3.2. Expected Results From Four Different Sales and Operations Plans

	Unbiased forecast				Linearly scaled forecast			
	Planned quantity (units)	Planned revenue ($)	Fill rate (%)	Expected profit ($)	Planned quantity (units)	Planned revenue ($)	Fill rate (%)	Expected profit ($)
Product A	500	5,500	88	1,799	698	7,674	94	2,057
Product B	700	4,200	88	788	977	5,860	95	544
Product C	800	3,200	90	647	1,116	4,465	98	673
Total	2,000	12,900		3,235	2,791	18,000		3,274

	Marginal allocation				Unconstrained solution			
	Planned quantity (units)	Planned revenue ($)	Fill rate (%)	Expected profit ($)	Planned quantity (units)	Planned revenue ($)	Fill rate (%)	Expected profit ($)
Product A	1,056	11,616	98	2,260	1,665	18,315	100	2,328
Product B	541	3,246	80	802	600	3,600	84	811
Product C	787	3,148	90	643	1,027	4,108	96	76
Total	2,384	18,010		3,705	3,292	26,023		3,815

would not be recommended because of the low reliability of the demand estimate at the far end of the demand distribution.

This simple example serves to illustrate that uniform scaling of an unbiased forecast to achieve a prespecified overall revenue target can lead to a poor sales and operations plan. And yet this is a common approach that many companies follow. Scaling based on an estimate of marginal profit is better, but implementing such an approach requires knowledge of the demand distributions, which are usually known only in rough approximation if at all. Also, in the face of supply constraints, even scaling based on marginal profit will not necessarily lead to a good result.

So while uniform scaling of an unbiased forecast to reach a revenue target may not be desirable, finding a better analytical approach can be a challenge. However, the S&OP process is the appropriate place for deciding what degree of revenue scaling is appropriate and how the revenue scaling should be achieved. In many situations, a lower revenue target can lead to higher expected profit, especially if the product mix is altered. While some people might argue that a higher revenue target is worth chasing because of potentially increased market share, others might just as well argue that the higher revenue target is unrealistic and will lead to inventory overage and price reductions to reduce the excess supply. Both perspectives are credible, and the S&OP process provides the right forum to hash out differences of opinion and reach a sound decision. By imposing an often arbitrary revenue target on the S&OP process, management is short-circuiting the process and undermining its influence within the organization.

Incorporating Supply and Resource Constraints

One of the biggest challenges in the S&OP process is addressing supply and resource constraints that affect how much product can be supplied in a limited time frame. Supply constraints are usually unanticipated shortages in raw material or parts that preclude supplying the desired quantity of all products. Resource constraints can take a number of forms including limits on available plant or equipment capacity, manpower, or working capital. Virtually every company experiences supply and resource constraints regularly, even if the specific constraints that arise may not always be the same.

The basic difficulty in coping with supply and resource constraints is that it is rarely obvious which products should get first dibs on constrained supply or resources, as the following simple example demonstrates (the relevant information for this example is summarized in Table 3.3). A factory produces two products on four work centers. Product 1 has an average selling price of $90, while product 2 has an average selling price of $100. The raw material cost per unit of product 1 is $45; for product 2, it is $40. To produce a unit of product 1 requires 15 minutes on work center A, 15 minutes on work center B, 15 minutes on work center C, and 25 minutes on work center D. To produce a unit of product 2 requires 10 minutes on work center A, 35 minutes on work center B, 5 minutes on work center C, and 14 minutes on work center D. Each work center is available 2,400 minutes per week. The fixed cost for operating the factory per week, including labor and capital, is $5,000. There is a maximum demand of 100 units per week for product 1 and 50 units per week for product 2. The deceptively simple problem is to figure out how much of each product to produce each week in order to maximize profit, without exceeding the maximum demand for either product and without exceeding the capacity of any of the work centers.

One way to approach the problem is to follow a profit-maximization procedure and produce as much of the more profitable product as possible until either a work center is fully utilized or the maximum quantity of the product is produced. Any remaining capacity is then allocated to the less profitable product. Following this logic, you would produce the maximum of 50 units of product 2 (it being the most profitable at $60/unit,

Table 3.3. Data for Simple Production Planning Problem

	Product 1	Product 2
Selling price ($)	90	100
Raw material cost ($)	45	40
Max. weekly sales (units)	100	50
Minutes per unit on work center A	15	10
Minutes per unit on work center B	15	35
Minutes per unit on work center C	15	5
Minutes per unit on work center D	25	14
Note: All workstations available 2,400 minutes/week; $5,000 fixed costs per week for labor and capital.		

excluding fixed costs), which leaves 1,900 minutes remaining per week on work center A, 650 minutes remaining on work center B, 2,150 minutes remaining on work center C, and 1,700 minutes remaining on work center D. This remaining capacity allows for 43 units of product 1 to be produced, at which point work center B's time has been fully utilized and no more units of either product can be produced. Producing 50 units of product 1 and 43 units of product 2 per week leads to a profit of $50 \times 60 + 43 \times 45 - 5,000 = \$-65$. So following this logic, the solution leads to a loss of $65 per week—not too promising.

The problem with the profit maximization procedure logic is that it does not take into consideration the "cost" of using a finite resource—namely, the time available on the work centers. An alternative ad hoc approach that tries to address this shortcoming is a bottleneck argument that says that you should allocate time based on which work center is the most constrained—that is, the bottleneck work center. Then, the reasoning goes, products should be produced based on maximizing the profit generated per minute spent on the bottleneck work center. When the maximum demand for each product is produced (100/week for product 1 and 50/week for product 2), this leads to requiring 2,000 minutes on work center A, 3,250 minutes on work center B, 1,750 minutes on work center C, and 3,200 minutes on work center D. Since work center B requires the most time, it is designated as the bottleneck work center. The profit generated per minute spent on work center B for product 1 is $\$45/15 = \$3$; for product 2, it is $\$60/35 = \$1.71$. So from this perspective, it makes sense to produce as much of product 1 as possible to maximize the profit per unit of time on the bottleneck work center. This leads to producing 96 units per week of product 1, which utilizes the full amount of time on work center D. Therefore, none of product 2 can be produced. The resulting profit is $\$45 \times 96 - 5,000 = -\$680$. So the bottleneck argument leads to an even worse solution, from a profitability perspective, than the profit maximization procedure.

Part of the problem with the bottleneck approach is that the determination of the bottleneck depends on how much you assume is produced of each product—in this case, the assumption was that you produced 100/week of product 1 and 50/week of product 2. If we assumed a different mix, a different work center would be designated as the bottleneck. But designating any other work center as the bottleneck leads to a higher profitability per unit of time on the bottleneck machine for product 2, which leads to the same solution as the profit maximization procedure, —namely, production of 50 units of product 2 and 43 units of product 1.

Both the profit maximization procedure and the bottleneck approach are examples of resource allocation heuristics sometimes referred to as "myopic" or "greedy" procedures because they always produce as much of one product as possible based on some metric until a constraint is reached and then switch to the next most desirable product (based on the metric), and so on until either all products have been allocated to their maximum quantity or resource constraints have been reached. In the profit maximization procedure, the metric utilized is profit per unit; in the bottleneck approach, the metric utilized is profit per minute of time on the bottleneck work center.

Greedy procedures work well in many circumstances, but this example shows that they have their limitations and don't always work well. To see why, you can solve this problem as a linear program (using Excel's solver, for example) to explicitly find the solution that maximizes profit per week. The solution is to produce 76 units of product 1 and 36 units of product, which yields a profit of $45 \times 76 + 60 \times 36 - 5,000 = \$580$. Neither of the previous greedy procedures comes close to achieving this solution or level of profitability.

The point of this example is to show that even in a simple case where resource constraints are present, the problem of finding a solution that maximizes profit is nontrivial. Ad hoc solution approaches cannot be relied upon to produce consistently good solutions. Difficulties mount when constraints become more complex and when demand and supply variability is present. So the challenge for any S&OP process is how to find a good solution to the problem of how much to produce given an unconstrained forecast, some degree of variability around the unconstrained forecast, and a variety of resource and supply constraints.

Often, in the face of this complexity, companies do not even bother to incorporate resource constraints into the S&OP process. Rather, they assume, within perhaps some reasonable bounds, that there is enough raw material supply and production and distribution capacity to meet the S&OP plan. The plan is then passed to manufacturing, distribution, and procurement and may then be run through an MRP, DRP, or finite capacity scheduling system. If there is a supply or resource shortage, it will turn up at this point and operations will be forced to scramble to overcome the constraints, possibly at great incremental cost to the company. In fact, many companies view these incremental costs—such as expediting costs or overtime costs—as sunk costs so don't even see explicitly the cost of ignoring these constraints in the S&OP process.

So pervasive is this approach that it has been given an informal name among manufacturing and procurement personnel: "load and chase," as in, load the S&OP plan into the Enterprise Resource Planning (ERP) system, and if there are shortages (which invariably, there are), chase the shortfall in supply. But by not explicitly taking into account supply shortages and resource constraints in the S&OP decision process, companies potentially pay a heavy price in the form of expediting costs, reduced service levels, and suboptimal product mix decisions, as the preceding simple example demonstrates.

The problem is how to incorporate these constraints explicitly into the S&OP process. The best way to do this is to utilize decision support tools that can help S&OP decision makers quickly assess the impact of S&OP plans on resource constraints, either by recommending S&OP plans that respect supply and capacity constraints or that report constraint violations of a candidate plan. The underpinning of these decision support tools is resource allocation optimization technology—for example, linear programming, mixed integer programming, stochastic optimization, and nonlinear optimization. A wide variety of commercial software—generally referred to under the rubric "advanced planning and scheduling (APS) software"—exists that incorporates this technology.[8] Unfortunately, many of these solutions suffer from four drawbacks that have hampered their effective use in supporting the S&OP process:

- They suffer from the "black box" syndrome, meaning that users are unfamiliar with the underlying technology and do not understand or trust the solutions that are generated, which may not make intuitive sense.
- The models tend to be highly detailed and data intensive, requiring significant effort to keep the models up to date.
- The software is not designed to support real-time decision support. Because of the complexity of the models, run times for generating a scenario can take hours or more and the

software itself is often awkward to use to perform rapid what-if experiments. Just changing the input data to analyze an alternative scenario can require significant time and effort.

- The software has not been explicitly designed to support the S&OP process but rather is intended more as an execution system, like an MRP system. The level of detail at which the MRP system is configured is usually far greater than what is required at the S&OP level. Anyone who has tried to use an MRP or APS system to run what-if scenarios knows the frustrations of such an exercise.

So these APS solutions are not usually the right choice for supporting the highly dynamic and consensus-driven nature of the S&OP process. Fortunately, it is no longer necessary to rely on packaged commercial software to support your S&OP process: You can construct your own using widely available relatively inexpensive software tools that enable the rapid construction of custom-configured decision support solutions.[9] This approach allows you to create a solution that is tailored to address the specific challenges that your company faces in its S&OP process usually at a total cost of ownership far lower than the cost of purchasing and maintaining a packaged software solution.

In the absence of any of software tools to support the S&OP process, it is difficult but not impossible to incorporate resource constraints into the S&OP process. A starting point is to at least make the constraints explicit in the form of reports that show how much supply or capacity is available, especially for the raw material or resources that are typically constrained. When an S&OP plan is proposed, it should be evaluated to see if any resource constraints are violated. If so, either the plan can be modified or actions can be initiated early on—such as procuring additional supply from alternative suppliers—to alleviate the constraints.

Dealing With Excess Supply

A practical issue that frequently arises in the S&OP process is how to deal with excess supply of parts, raw material, or finished goods that have been acquired but are either at end of life or are simply sitting unused because demand has dried up. Normally, in these circumstances, the unbiased forecast for the products utilizing the parts or raw materials is far below the available supply. How should the S&OP process deal with this excess supply? If it is ignored, the chances of actually selling it are greatly diminished because visibility to the supply will be lost and sales will have little motivation to try to sell it. On the other hand, if the S&OP decision makers decide to increase the sales and operations plan to reflect available supply, the risk is that other products that are more likely to sell may get short shrift. As a result, you may end up with a lot of inventory of products with no demand and not enough supply for the products with high demand.

Though this is never a desirable situation to be in, the right response is to highlight the available supply of these products in the S&OP plan but at the same time to segregate these products in a separate category to be treated and tracked differently from others. In one large computer manufacturing company, the category is labeled as "liability product" and the appearance of products in this category in the S&OP plan is a signal to undertake demand conditioning activities to try to sell the excess product, not to drive additional supply for the product.

Relation to Demand Conditioning

The S&OP plan should be used as a guide by sales to figure out where to focus sales. If the output of the S&OP process says that the company is positioning itself to supply 10,000 units of a given product, the sales force should use this information to figure out how best to sell 10,000 units. This may entail the ability to quickly take actions to increase the chances of selling the items, including price reductions, promotions, and sales incentives. These activities—collectively referred to as demand conditioning—are intended to have the result that the likelihood of selling to the S&OP plan is increased.

When the S&OP process occurs at a product family level, some complexity arises due to product mix issues within each family. The target availability of different SKUs within each family may be different and this information should be utilized by sales in steering customers to different products within a family. Ideally, sales will have instant access to up-to-date information on availability of parts or SKUs and can use this information to steer customers to those parts or SKUs within the family that are in stock and available to sell. This available-to-promise information can serve as a valuable demand conditioning tool. Even if accurate timely information is not available to sales personnel, they can make use of the different target service levels as a tool to set delivery expectations with customers.

Structure of the S&OP Process

Steps in the S&OP process

While the precise nature and set of activities comprising the S&OP process will vary substantially depending on many specific aspects of a company—the nature of demand and how customers are served, the lead time for products and the kinds of supply constraints it typically confronts—an S&OP process should generally include the following steps:

- Estimate demand variability. Using approaches outlined earlier, this step can be done using forecast accuracy data, historical sales, or obtaining bounds on forecasts from the forecast process. This step can be assigned to the forecasting function of the organization or to S&OP personnel.
- Generate candidate sales and operations plans based on the unbiased forecast, demand variability, and supply constraints. This activity can be carried out using decision support software or manually. The result should be at least two or three different potential plans. For each candidate plan, report on
  - ° supply level and anticipated coverage of demand,
  - ° service-level targets by SKU or component,
  - ° inventory targets.
- Report metrics on the previous S&OP cycle, including service levels (attained vs. target), inventory levels (attained vs. target), sales (actual vs. sales and operations plan), operating margins, and expedite costs.
- Conduct S&OP interlock meeting. This is a meeting with representatives from sales, marketing, finance, operations, product development, procurement, and the general manager of the business to select a sales and operations plan.
- Publish the sales and operations plan and management metrics.

The cadence of this process should be a function of how much time the process takes (both in elapsed time and in resource expenditure) and how frequently the sales and operations plan needs to be updated. Most companies conduct this process monthly but allow for course corrections when needed. For example, if a major supply disruption becomes apparent at some point during a month, it may trigger an S&OP cycle to occur before the next official S&OP cycle is due to start. This cycle may be abbreviated (certain steps may be omitted) but it is important to have the capability to respond to changing events as they occur and not be tied to a rigid schedule that might delay a timely response to a market altering event.

An important step in the S&OP process is the interlock meeting. Its purpose is to decide, among candidate plans that have been prepared beforehand, which one to select as the official sales and operations plan. The candidate plans should all have been generated with input from the S&OP interlock participants and the participants should have reviewed all the candidate plans prior to the meeting. If participants are properly prepared, the meeting should consist of debate on the relative merits of the different candidate plans—what the trade-offs are and the impact of each plan on overall business performance. In most cases, the most promising plan will be evident quite quickly and this is the one that will be adopted. In some cases, valuable insight can be obtained through discussions among the participants and may cause the decision to be swayed to an alternate plan.

Because the S&OP interlock involves making critical business trade-offs among multiple objectives in the face of uncertainty about demand and supply, and must take into consideration a variety of supply and resource constraints, it makes sense that an effective interlock meeting is one in which all the key stakeholders of a company—sales, marketing, finance, operations, product development, procurement, as well as the general manager—are tasked with jointly arriving at a decision about how to best position the company to meet future demand. The representatives of each function participating in the S&OP interlock should have sufficient stature within the company that their viewpoints and decisions carry weight. No particular function should have undue influence on the outcome and senior management should not be allowed to arbitrarily override the output after the interlock meeting is complete, by, for example, imposing arbitrary revenue targets. Without such controls, the process will be undermined by a lack of confidence in the result and will gradually become irrelevant.

What's the Right Level of Product, Geography, and Time Granularity for the S&OP Process?

In their book on the S&OP process, Ling and Goddard write that "Sales and Operations Planning is done on an 'aggregate' or 'family' level, and covers a sufficient span of time to make sure that the necessary resources will be available."[10] The reason for planning at a product family level is that carrying out the process at a more detailed level will lead to too much complexity. However, if the products that make up each family have significantly different characteristics and components, there is a real risk that planning at a family level will cause supply and service-level problems due to product mix issues. The same issue may exist at the geography level too.

To illustrate the problem, consider a computer manufacturer that generates an unbiased forecast at a family level and then carries out the S&OP process at the same family level. After the S&OP plan has been determined, it is converted into a supply requirement statement at the part level. The problem is that the conversion into a part supply statement requires knowing precisely the parts that make up machines in each family—that is, the bill of material. However, since each family can have a large variety of configurations, there is no single bill of material for a family. Machines within a family may require different processors, different kinds of memory, or different network cards. If the S&OP plan calls for supplying 1,000 units of product family X, how does this translate to the number of processors to procure if the 10 models that make up the family utilize 10 different processors? How many processors of each type should be procured? Should planners look at past consumption to figure out the right percent to procure of each processor? Should procurement get more than 1,000 processors to protect against the variability in the product mix even though the sales and operations plan stipulates to plan for only 1,000 units of sales?

What should be apparent from this example is that the sales and operations plan provided at the family level is lacking key information that is needed to carry out the plan. If the sales and operations plan stipulates supplying 1,000 units of family X, then it leaves too much to the imagination of manufacturing and procurement personnel to decide exactly how to supply these 1,000 units. Their decision will be made without guidance from the S&OP process and though their intentions may be good, they will be making a key decision without input from the key S&OP stakeholders. In a very real sense, the sales and operations plan stipulating that 1,000 units of the product family be supplied becomes irrelevant and superfluous: The procurement and manufacturing personnel become focused solely on how to maintain or chase enough supply to meet demand, regardless of the sales and operations plan. Also, sales will likely be making its own assumptions about what the 1,000 units of available supply for family X means, and these assumptions are unlikely to coincide with the decisions made by procurement and manufacturing. The products they end up selling may or may not have any relationship to the parts that procurement is purchasing—an outcome that the S&OP process is specifically intended to avoid.

Converting the family-level S&OP plan to a parts requirement plan effectively requires another layer of forecasting—how much of each component is required given a family-level forecast. And implicit in this conversion is some measure of protection against product mix variability. Arguably, forecasting the component usage within a family is at least as hard as forecasting at the family level. And yet, isn't the purpose of the S&OP process to align all the functions within a company to an agreed on supply level? If so, there is a key piece of guidance missing from the S&OP process in this case: What level of supply availability should be targeted at the part level given the uncertainty of the product mix? If the S&OP process occurs at an aggregate level, it is incumbent for the process to provide this level of guidance or the result will almost surely be excess inventory of certain components and poor service levels—the usual signs of a systemic mismatch of supply and demand.

So if the S&OP process occurs at a family level—and there are good reasons to do so in order to reduce decision-making complexity—then a key output of the S&OP process is to provide direction in the form of service-level targets that procurement and manufacturing should attempt to achieve, either at the individual SKU or part level, or for groups of SKUs or groups of parts. These service-level targets either should be consistent with the family-level plan or should call out explicitly that the supply of parts will need to exceed the family-level plan in total in order to meet the desired service-level targets. In the previous example, the sales and operations plan might say to supply 1,000 units for family X. In addition, it should stipulate the target availability for different processors used by this family. For example, processors 1–4 might be designated as "A" items whose target in-stock rate might be set at 99%, processors 5–7 might be designated as "B" items with a target in-stock rate of 95%, and processors 8–10 might be designated as "C" items with a target in-stock rate of 90%. Without these targets, the sales and operations plan is under-determined and will almost certainly lead to different functions making different assumptions about supply availability and working at cross-purposes—exactly what the S&OP process is intended to avoid. The target service levels can then be utilized in the inventory planning process to determine the stocking level of each part. Also, the information can be used by sales to determine the service level to offer to customers based on the product configuration the customer chooses. Finally, the service-level targets can be utilized to track performance of the S&OP process over time by comparing the actual achieved service levels to the targets. When these targets are consistently over- or underachieved, a root cause analysis can be undertaken to understand and address the problems.

When the S&OP process stipulates service-level targets, it should be done with some knowledge of the impact that these targets will have on inventory levels. In the previous example, if the target in-stock rate is set at 99% for processors 1–4, the S&OP process should understand that the implication for setting the in-stock rate at this level will be to plan for enough safety stock to meet this service level given demand variability and lead times. How this is achieved in practice is the role of inventory and supply planning, taken up in chapter 4, but the S&OP process should have an approximate understanding of the impact of the service-level targets on inventory levels. Otherwise, the S&OP decision will not be based on facts about how much the plan will realistically cost.

To gain this understanding, S&OP personnel can utilize one of two approaches. One possibility is to ask inventory planners how much inventory is required to meet a given set of service-level targets at the SKU or part level. In the previous example, inventory planners might say that to achieve an in-stock rate of 99% for processors 1–4, given demand variability and lead times, requires approximately 8 weeks of supply for processors 1 and 2 and 12 weeks of supply for processors 3 and 4. Likewise, to meet the 95% in-stock rate for processors 5–7 will require approximately 7 weeks of supply for each processor. And to meet the 90% in-stock rate for processors 8–10 might require 9 weeks for processor 8 and 5 weeks each for processors 9 and 10. When these weeks of supply are converted to units needed to support the sale of 1,000 units of supply, the total may far exceed the 1,000 total planned for product family X. What is to be done? It depends. If the risk of obsolescence is low and price takedowns are small, the S&OP personnel may decide that the level of supply needed to support the service-level targets are worth the price. On the other hand, if, as with most computer components, obsolescence risk is high and price takedowns are generally frequent, the decision may be to lower the service-level targets to lower the inventory risk.

An alternative approach, which is less common because the formulation and solution of the problem is difficult, is to treat the family-level sales and operations plan as a constraint and figure out how to allocate supply among the different parts in order to maximize a measure of service-level attainment. To use the computer example again, the question might be how many processors of the different types should be procured so that the total supply of processors does not exceed 1,000 in order to maximize a weighted sum of the in-stock rate of the processors, where the weights are the expected demand for each processor. This is a stochastic optimization problem, and its formulation and solution is not yet a standard capability of any packaged software solution. However, formulating and solving the problem using one of many widely availability modeling environments is possible, though not by any means simple. By solving this problem for a variety of different family-level values, the S&OP stakeholders can get a sense of what in-stock rates will be achieved at the SKU or part level given a family-level plan and can make a more informed decision about what the family-level plan should be.

Outputs: Sales and Operations Plan, Service-Level Goals, and Inventory Targets

The S&OP process results in a sales and operations plan that consists of three essential components:

1. The planned supply of products, most often stipulated at a family level by month and by geography.
2. The target service level specified at the SKU or part level.
3. An estimate of the required inventory dollars needed to achieve the planned supply at the target service level.

In many companies, only the first output is recognized as the responsibility of the S&OP process. But as we have seen, if this is the only output and it is specified at a product family level, then not enough detail has been specified to allow for proper execution of the plan. By specifying target service levels for groups of SKUs or groups of components, this issue is addressed.

The final output—inventory dollars required to meet the planned supply at the target service level—is important both for financial planning and as an S&OP objective. By making this explicit, the company ensures that all S&OP participants are aware of the inventory commitment needed to meet the supply plan. It should be clear that the inventory dollars needed to meet the supply plan is not just the cost of goods to supply the family-level sales and operations plan. Depending on the target service levels that are stipulated, the target inventory levels could be substantially higher. For example, if the family-level sales and operations plan specifies 1,000 units but there are 10 different processors that can be utilized in the 1,000 units and the service-level target for all the processors is 95% availability, this will drive significantly more than 1,000 processors in inventory. How much more is a function of the demand variability for each processor as well as its lead time. The standard deviations of demand estimated as part of the S&OP process can be utilized to estimate demand variability at the part or SKU level, which can then be used to determine an estimate of required inventory to meet the service-level targets. While it is ultimately the responsibility of the inventory planners to determine the quantity of inventory needed to meet the target service levels, it is nonetheless important for the S&OP process to create an initial estimate of how much inventory is required as a way to assess which plan to go forward with.

S&OP Process-Management Metrics

To be effective, the S&OP process needs to have accountability in the form of clear metrics and objectives that are tracked and published.

The right metrics involve a mix of service level and revenue attainment, working capital targets, profit margins, and expedite costs. Reporting of performance of previous S&OP cycles should show the variance between the planned supply and the actual demand, achieved service levels versus targets, and actual inventory levels versus targets. Specific considerations in developing the right set of management metrics include the following:

1. *Service-level metrics.* Reports should include both customer-oriented service-level metrics, such as percent of customer orders received or shipped on time and more internally focused metrics such as out-of-stock rates of parts in manufacturing or distribution facilities. The reports should show both the achieved service levels and the target service levels and should highlight cases where the actual service levels are significantly above or below the target.

2. *Sales attainment.* This should provide a comparison between what sales were achieved relative to the sales and operations plan. Significant discrepancies should be highlighted. It is also useful to include the unbiased forecast in this comparison as an additional point of comparison. This metric should be calculated at the same level of granularity at which the sales and operations plan is generated. Note that if sales come in below the sales and operations plan, this is not necessarily an indication of a problem. If the S&OP decision was to position supply at the 95th percentile of the demand distribution, there is a 95% chance that sales will come in below the plan. Of course, if demand conditioning activities are really effective, then the probability of achieving the plan should be greatly increased.

3. *Inventory metrics.* These metrics should provide a comparison between the actual inventory levels and turnover and the S&OP targets. If the actual inventory levels exceed the targets but service levels for those parts or SKUs are either not being met or just being met, further investigation may be warranted. It may be simply that the inventory targets were based on demand variability assumptions that were too low. Inventory in these reports should include both company-owned finished goods, raw material, and work in process, as well as liability inventory—for example, inventory that may be held by suppliers or third parties but for which the company has liability.

4. *Expedite cost metrics.* These metrics should capture all costs incurred due to "heroics" undertaken to meet customer demand. Cost categories include expedited inbound freight on raw material, labor costs associated with chasing additional supply, premiums paid for parts or goods bought outside ordinary terms and conditions, expedited outbound logistics costs, and transshipments between company sites that are done on an exception basis (not a part of normal business). If possible, the metrics should differentiate between costs incurred to meet demand that was within the sales and operations plan and those incurred to meet demand beyond the sales and operations plan. This distinction helps in two ways. First, if significant expedite expense is incurred to meet demand within the sales and operations plan, this fact may indicate a problem with the way the sales and operations plan is being communicated or utilized. Over time, expedite costs for demand within the sales and operations plan should decline significantly once it is being monitored. Second, knowing the expedite expense incurred to satisfy demand beyond the sales and operations plan should influence future S&OP decisions. If that expense is very high, it may drive higher sales and operations plans to lower the chances of incurring those costs, though this needs to be balanced against the added inventory risk and costs.

5. *Operating margins.* While many factors influence operating margins, effective S&OP should, over time, result in increasing operating margins, as the company makes better decisions about positioning supply and becomes more effective at selling to that supply. It is therefore a justifiable management metric to track as part of the S&OP process.

While many of these metrics are affected by activities outside the S&OP process, including them is important as a means to ensure end-to-end accountability.

Investing in Improved Sales and Operations Planning

The telltale signs that an S&OP process is not working properly (whether it is referred to by name or not) are poor service levels, high expediting costs, low inventory turnover, and low operating margins—the critical indicators of poor demand-supply matching. The opportunities to improve S&OP—and thereby improve these metrics—are usually significant. The challenges are identifying what needs to change in the process, determining what software tools or other key enablers are needed to make these changes, and estimating the impact of these changes.

To figure out what changes are necessary to the process, a good starting point is to map out the process in some detail. Note if any of the steps described earlier are missing, if any outputs are missing, and if the right metrics are being reported. If key metrics are missing, it may be worthwhile to undertake an analysis to calculate these key metrics, which may require a data collection effort. The end result of this assessment is an understanding of the gaps in the existing process and a baseline of current performance.

Certain steps of the S&OP process can be carried out more quickly and more effectively with the use of proper analytical software tools. In particular, software can greatly facilitate two steps in the process—analyzing demand and forecast data to assess demand variability and generating candidate sales and operations plans. Many inexpensive software tools are available to help with distribution fitting and statistical analysis of demand data.[11] Deploying software that can assist with the generation of candidate sales and operations plans is more difficult and more expensive. Within the last 10 years, software vendors have begun to offer packaged solutions that claim to support the S&OP process.[12] Investing in one of these solutions may be worthwhile, but before doing so, you would be wise to invest time in developing a prototype decision support solution and conducting a pilot of the S&OP process using the prototype. Building a prototype decision support tool can be done inexpensively today by leveraging sophisticated software modeling tools. While you may end up discarding this model, it can serve as the basis for defining the requirements of a commercial decision support solution or a more robust custom solution. This procedure is much more effective than the traditional request-for-proposal (RFP) approach that many companies follow and leads to a much higher degree of learning.

The ultimate question about what kind of return you can expect from investing in improved S&OP is always difficult to answer because it depends on how well your company currently addresses the challenges of S&OP. One concrete estimate of cost savings can be obtained by looking honestly at the costs you currently expend on expediting orders or raw materials. Most often, expediting is the result of poor planning—to amend a common saying, poor planning on your part does not constitute an emergency on my part, except when you are my boss. Improved S&OP should result in a significant reduction in expedite costs, and this reduction goes straight to the bottom line. Of course, the value of improved customer service levels, improved inventory turnover, and increased operating margins should not be overlooked and may in fact be far greater than the reduction in expedite costs, but these are much harder to estimate before any improvement activities are undertaken.

CHAPTER 4

Inventory and Supply Planning

Plans are only good intentions unless they immediately degenerate into hard work.

—Peter Drucker

At the conclusion of the sales and operations planning (S&OP) process, a sales and operations plan consisting of sales targets, service-level targets, and inventory targets has been established. At this point, planners are tasked with operationalizing the sales and operations plan. This means figuring out when to place orders on suppliers, what the size of those orders should be, where products should be produced, when manufacturing should begin production, and where inventory should be stored and in what form.

This chapter focuses on the challenges that planners face once the sales and operations plan has been established. If the S&OP process has been performed at an appropriate level of detail and has incorporated supply and resource constraints, then the planning activities are manageable, though many challenges still remain. If the S&OP process has not provided enough guidance, planning activities become less clear, which often leads to inconsistent decision making, second guessing, and redundancy.

The task of transforming the sales and operations plan into an operational plan is the responsibility of planning personnel throughout the company who are variously identified as inventory planners, production planners, supply planners, promotion planners, and distribution planners. Some companies have production and supply planners but no inventory planners. Some have inventory planners but no distribution planners. That does not mean inventory planning does not occur in the former group or that distribution planning does not occur in the latter. It simply means that planners with other job titles are performing those functions. How these activities are labeled is relatively inconsequential as long as groups within the company understand where planning responsibilities reside. For the sake of simplicity, I refer collectively to these planning activities as inventory and supply planning.

Many books, including standard operations management textbooks and more advanced operations modeling books, cover the concepts and techniques of inventory and supply planning.[1] While most of this material has been well documented, not much attention has been given to making the connection between the S&OP process and these planning activities. Most operations management textbooks do not even mention the S&OP process. As a result, students of operations management may be forgiven for thinking that S&OP and operations management exist in separate spheres with little or no connection between them. Yet in order for the S&OP process to have any practical relevance in the company, the linkages between it and inventory and supply planning need to be clearly delineated. Spelling out these linkages is one of the principle objectives of this chapter. I also touch on a number of practical planning challenges that arise in this context that operations management textbooks typically don't address.

A Simple Inventory Management Problem

To understand the kinds of problems that planners face in translating the sales and operations plan into an operational plan, it's helpful to start with the simple example of an auto parts distributor that serves customers out of regional warehouses. Suppose the company has conducted its latest S&OP process and for a certain family of oil filters, consisting of 10 individual stock-keeping units (SKUs), has set a target in-stock rate of 98% for all warehouses and therefore is prepared to position supply to be at the 98th percentile of the demand distribution. The S&OP process has estimated that the average amount of inventory required to have on hand in order to meet that service level, given the historical demand variability for these oil filters is approximately 2 weeks' worth, though it is up to the inventory planners to determine the right amount of inventory at the SKU and warehouse level to achieve this target in-stock rate. The warehouses generally place replenishment orders with suppliers once per week (usually on Mondays), and the lead time for the oil filters, from the time the orders are placed to the time the orders are received at the warehouses, is about 2 weeks. Since orders are placed once per week, the orders are intended to cover approximately 1 week of demand. The warehouses operate 6 days per week, shipping out orders from customers and receiving replenishments from suppliers. The inventory planner must decide each week how big an order to place for oil filters in order to maintain a 98% in-stock rate.

Relationship Between S&OP and Inventory and Supply Planning

It is worthwhile to point out exactly what information the S&OP process has transmitted to the inventory planners in this simple scenario. Note that the S&OP process has not dictated exactly what the replenishment policy for oil filters should be—that is left to the inventory planners to figure out. Rather, the sales and operations planners have appropriately stated that the inventory planners should target a 98% in-stock rate for all SKUs in this family. They then allow the inventory planners to do their jobs to figure out how best to achieve that target service level.

The S&OP process has also indicated that the 98% in-stock rate should be achievable, based on estimates of demand variability, by holding approximately 2 weeks of supply on hand. How did the S&OP process arrive at this number, and should the inventory planners be held to it? The S&OP personnel calculated this value by performing the following approximate calculation based on information gathered during the S&OP process. Because orders are placed every week, if there were no variability in demand and no variability in lead time, you would have on hand at the beginning of each week exactly 1 week of supply—the amount needed to fill demand for the coming week (subsequent weeks' demand would be replenished at the start of each week). Based on the analysis of demand variability that the S&OP personnel have carried out, they have characterized weekly demand variability for these oil filters as having a coefficient of variation of 0.3. To achieve 98% coverage of demand for a week will require approximately an additional 0.6 weeks of supply based on assuming the weekly demand follows a normal distribution. Allowing for some additional inventory due to other factors, such as lead time variability, as well as being conservative in their estimates, they round the number of weeks of inventory required to meet the 98% in-stock rate to 2 weeks.

This is a back-of-the-envelope estimate, and the inventory planners should not be held to this value. It is only intended as a guideline, and the inventory planners should be prepared to explain any significant deviations from this value. But ultimately, it is the inventory planners who are responsible for determining the best way to achieve the 98% in-stock rate. As long as they can defend their approach, the S&OP personnel should accept the outcome. For example, suppose inventory levels turn out to be closer to 3 weeks, and the inventory planners explain this higher level as necessary due to significantly higher variability in demand. As long as the inventory planners have the data to back up their claims, the S&OP personnel should accept this higher level of inventory. Or suppose the inventory planners decide that it makes more sense to order oil filters every 2 weeks as opposed to every week in order to save on fixed ordering and shipping costs. This will result in higher average on-hand inventory levels. As long as the inventory planners can justify this change by showing that the reduction in ordering and shipping costs more than offsets the increased inventory holding costs, the S&OP personnel should accept this change and should incorporate this information in subsequent S&OP cycles.

Potential Disconnect Between Inventory and Supply Planning and the S&OP Process

A common problem in supply chain planning occurs when the direction set by the S&OP process is not followed by inventory and supply planners. This does not happen because the inventory and supply planners are stubborn and think they know better than the S&OP process. It's most often because the S&OP process is performed at too high a level to be of use for inventory and supply planning.

To illustrate how this might happen, suppose the S&OP process in the oil filter example, rather than stipulating a target in-stock rate for the 10 oil filters to be 98%, only specified that the aggregate sales and operations plan for the family of 10 oil filters was, say, 5,500 units for the current month, 6,700 units for the next month, and 7,900 units for the following month. Based on this information, the inventory planners need to figure out how to allocate this aggregate plan among the 10 different SKUs. The problem is that they do not have adequate guidance to make this decision. It could be split based proportionally on the unbiased forecast for each oil filter, but such an approach will not necessarily lead to a desirable allocation. Faced with this circumstance, inventory planners typically end up effectively ignoring the aggregate sales and operations plan and arrive at their own calculation of how much inventory to plan for based on an explicit or implicit target service level that they establish. On the other hand, if the sales and operations plan specifies, in addition, that a 98% in-stock rate is to be achieved, then the aggregate plan becomes superfluous: The inventory planners can determine an inventory policy that will achieve a 98% service level given the unbiased forecast at the SKU level and an estimate of the SKU-level demand distribution. The aggregate sales and operations plan is not necessary to perform this calculation.

It should be clear from this example that the connection between the S&OP process and inventory and supply planning is precisely through the target service levels that are established during the S&OP process. If the S&OP process only specifies a family-level supply plan, inventory and supply planners are left with too little information to make an informed decision about how to implement the sales and operations plan. From the perspective of inventory and supply planning, the appropriate role for the sales and operations plan is to set customer-service-level targets. The role of inventory and supply planning is to figure out the most cost effective mechanism for achieving those service levels. If these roles are not properly understood, supply chain performance will suffer.

Inventory Planning 101

In order for the inventory planners to figure out how to achieve a 98% in-stock rate for the oil filters, they can rely, as a starting point, on well-documented inventory management theory. The standard textbook treatment of this problem is to determine a target inventory position needed to achieve a 98% in-stock rate, taking into consideration forecasted demand, demand variability, and lead time variability. The target inventory position stipulates the quantity of inventory that should be maintained on hand and on order to achieve the desired service level. A typical calculation of the target inventory position starts with the observation that the quantity of inventory that you purchase today will be utilized to satisfy 1 week's worth of demand starting in 2 weeks (i.e., after the order has been received). However, you may need to order less if the quantity of inventory that is currently on hand plus on order exceeds the quantity needed to meet demand at a 98% in-stock rate for the next 2 weeks. That is the quantity left over in inventory that can be utilized to supply additional demand beyond 2 weeks. On the other hand, you may need to order more if the current on-hand plus on-order quantity is insufficient to meet demand over the next 2 weeks.[2] So the standard reasoning is that you need to order a quantity that will bring the inventory position up to a level that will supply demand over the next 3 weeks at a 98% in-stock rate. This is usually expressed as the sum of two terms—the mean demand over the next 3 weeks (the lead time plus order coverage period, denoted in the following equation as P) plus the necessary number of standard deviations of the demand over this period above the mean needed to ensure that the in-stock rate will be met:

$$\text{Target inventory position} \equiv \mu_p + k\sigma_p.$$

In order to determine a value for k in this situation, you need to make an assumption about the distribution of demand over the next $P(=3)$ weeks. This is one key place in which estimates of the demand distribution obtained in the S&OP process are utilized. To achieve a 98% in-stock rate, the value of k should be set so that the target inventory position is equal to the 98th percentile of the demand distribution over P.

To continue with the oil filter example, suppose that at the start of the first week in March, the unbiased forecast of demand for a specific oil filter SKU at a warehouse serving the southwest U.S. region is 120 units for the current week, 150 units for the following week, and 180 units for the week after. Assuming that the S&OP process has estimated the coefficient of variation of weekly demand as 0.3 and that the distribution of weekly demand is normally distributed, the target inventory position at the start of the week would be calculated as follows:

$$\mu_p = 120 + 150 + 180 = 450$$

$$\sigma_p = ((120 * 0.3)^2 + (150 * 0.3)^2 + (180 * 0.3)^2)^{1/2} \approx 79$$

$$k = N^{-1}(0.98) \approx 2.05^3$$

Target inventory position $= 450 + 2.05 * 79 \approx 612$.

Using this target inventory position, a purchasing agent would review the current on-hand inventory in the warehouse plus the on-order inventory and compare this to the target inventory position. If the inventory position were below the target inventory position, the purchasing agent would place an order to bring the inventory position to at least 612 units. For example, suppose the current on-hand inventory is 100, and there is an outstanding purchase order (PO) for an additional 160 units due to arrive within 1 week. Then the purchasing agent would place an additional PO for 612 – 260 = 352 units.

While the target inventory position calculation is a reasonable starting point for achieving the target service level in this simple example, a number of complicating factors arise in practice. These complications are what make inventory and supply planning much more challenging than this example suggests. The remainder of this chapter is devoted to raising these issues and discussing methods to address them.

A Note About Inventory and Supply Planning Software Systems

In practice, the activities of the purchasing agent and the inventory planner in this example would be wholly or partially performed by software. A huge variety of software systems exist to automate the processes of inventory and supply planning both in distribution and in production settings. A significant challenge of inventory and supply planning today is navigating the software jungle: understanding the strengths and limitations of these software systems amid the cacophony of claims and making sound decisions on what systems provide the best value for your company. One objective of this chapter is to highlight some of these strengths and weaknesses.

Lot Size Restrictions, Volume Discounts, and Joint Replenishment

In the oil filter example, the order quantity determined from the target inventory position is whatever the difference is between the actual inventory position and the target when the order is placed, if the difference is positive. In most circumstances, this difference is not what is ordered. The reason is that most suppliers impose some kind of lot size restriction on orders. In the simplest case, this simply means that some logic must be performed to round the order quantity to a multiple of the lot size.

But other economic considerations come into play even if suppliers do not impose lot size restrictions. The fundamental economic trade-off in deciding an order quantity is the total per unit cost of obtaining inventory, which includes purchasing, shipping, and receiving costs versus the cost of holding inventory, which includes the financing cost of paying for the inventory, its storage cost, and the risks associated with holding inventory, such as shrinkage and obsolescence. The reason this is a trade-off is that, generally speaking, the cost of obtaining a unit of inventory decreases as the order quantity increases due to economies of scale, while the cost of holding inventory increases as the order quantity increases. The goal of the inventory planner should be to find an order quantity that balances these costs and minimizes the total cost of ownership of inventory. While this is straightforward in theory, the practical challenges of doing this calculation can be significant.

Most operations management textbooks have a section on the theory of the economic order quantity (EOQ). In the simplest setting, this theory establishes an expression for determining the order quantity that minimizes the total cost to procure the necessary supply of a product or component. The costs considered in this analysis are the cost of holding inventory and the fixed cost of placing replenishment orders. For the oil filter example, the EOQ model would be applied by first determining the annual demand for a given oil filter at a warehouse. Suppose that we estimate the annual demand at 6,000 filters per year. Then the model requires that we assess the fixed cost associated with placing an order with the supplier. This is a trickier number to estimate. But suppose for a moment that it is $10 per order. Finally, the model requires an estimate of the cost of holding a unit in inventory for 1 year. Generally, we can estimate this as the cost of capital for the company plus storage costs. A rough estimate of this number is twice the cost of capital. Suppose we estimate the holding cost of a unit of inventory at 20% of the purchase cost of $2.00 per filter. Then the EOQ is

$$EOQ = \sqrt{\frac{2K\lambda}{h}} = \sqrt{\frac{2*10*6000}{0.40}} \approx 548 \ .$$

No company I have ever worked with uses the EOQ formula to determine order quantities. The reason is not that the underlying model assumptions are usually violated (which happens to be true). Rather, it is that the fixed ordering cost is either ridiculously small or nearly impossible to estimate (or both). In most textbooks, the practical challenge of giving an honest accounting of the fixed ordering cost is not even mentioned. What costs are supposed to be captured? Is it the 15 seconds of labor that a purchasing agent spends reviewing the inventory position for this particular SKU before pressing a key to electronically transmit the purchase order? Is this labor cost really a fixed cost that would be recouped if the order was not placed? Is it the minuscule cost of storing and sending the electronic purchase order to the supplier? Even if both costs were considered, the EOQ formula would almost always yield an order quantity so small that it would violate the lot size restrictions of the supplier. So while the EOQ formula may have pedagogical value, its value in practice is limited.

The bigger problem with the EOQ model is that it ignores the most significant economies of scale that are realized as the order quantity increases—namely, the reduction in per-unit purchasing cost and inbound logistics cost. These are the costs that need to be captured in any thorough EOQ-like analysis. The discounts offered by suppliers can be complex and dynamic, so inventory planners need to be prepared to respond to forward buy opportunities as they arise. In addition, if the supplier is providing product FOB-source[4], the logistics costs associated with transporting from the source to the company storage location must be taken into account. These costs can be complex and dynamic as well, depending on what mode of transport is used, whether shipments are less-than-truckload (LTL) or full-truckload (TL), time of year, or a host of other factors. Just the task of collecting and maintaining all the data required to perform a comprehensive EOQ-like trade-off analysis can be time consuming and challenging.

Many purchasing and inventory management software systems have forward buy modules that will automatically recommend optimal order quantities given the price discounts offered by suppliers. Beware of using these modules without truly understanding the logic behind them. They may ignore certain costs or may not take into consideration certain logistics constraints, such as warehouse space limitations.

Even if these systems capture the total costs of ownership associated with a single SKU, they often ignore one of the most complex issues that arises in practice, that of joint or coordinated replenishment across multiple SKUs. Joint replenishment refers to the challenge of determining the order quantities for a set of SKUs when the purchase cost and inbound delivery cost is shared across these SKUs. To illustrate using the oil filter example, suppose all 10 oil filters in the family are obtained from the same supplier, and the supplier offers volume discounts based on the total number of oil filters purchased, not the number ordered of an individual SKU. Further, suppose that each order for oil filters is shipped as a single shipment and therefore that the inbound logistics costs are determined by the total volume of oil filters shipped, not the number of filters ordered of a particular SKU. Significant discounts on inbound logistics are realized if the shipment is TL, so it's worthwhile to consider ordering a quantity of oil filters that will fill an entire truckload even if the quantity required to reach the target inventory positions for all filters does not reach that level. A software module that calculates "optimal" order quantities for an individual SKU may recommend order quantities that may make no sense in aggregate if joint replenishment considerations are not taken into account.

Unfortunately, there is no simple EOQ formula to calculate optimal order quantities in the presence of complex price breaks and joint replenish constraints. On the other hand, determining optimal or near-optimal order quantities is not difficult using numerical approaches assuming data are available to assess the costs of different order configurations. The problem can be formulated as a nonlinear optimization problem and solved using numerical optimization methods or simply through less elegant but effective brute-force search. The capabilities of packaged software systems in this area are limited, and it may be cost effective to construct a custom configured solution, possibly leveraging generic optimization software. Above all, before attempting to construct a custom solution or deploy a packaged software solution, you should investigate the availability of data needed to drive a sound order quantity decision and establish a process for collecting and maintaining this data over time.

Without the right data, the fanciest algorithms for determining joint replenishment order quantities will fail.

Timing Issues

Maintaining the inventory position at the target level is a necessary, not sufficient, condition for meeting the service-level target. Timing of when replenishment orders arrive relative to when demand is realized has an important impact on both service levels and inventory levels. In the oil filter example, the 100 units that are on hand at the beginning of the week are not likely to meet the demand for the coming week, which is forecasted at 120 units. If all you look at is the inventory position, by ordering 352 units that are not due to arrive for 2 weeks, you are indeed bringing the inventory position up to its target, but you have not accomplished anything to alleviate the anticipated current week shortage. In fact, if demand is not typically backlogged, you may have overordered inventory because about 38 of the 352 units you are ordering is intended to cover the shortfall of inventory in the current week. To address the potential shortfall in the current week, you may need to either expedite a shipment from the supplier or transship some inventory from another warehouse.

By the same token, if demand for a product drops significantly, focusing only on maintaining the inventory position at or above the target may lead to holding excess inventory and to missed opportunities for canceling or postponing outstanding purchase orders. For example, suppose after you place the order for 352 oil filters, the demand for oil filters decreases substantially. The demand for this week only comes in at 50 units, and the forecast for subsequent weeks is reduced by 50%. The result will be that the target inventory position will be reduced (based on the reduced forecast), but the inventory position will remain above the target. The opportunity to delay or reduce the open purchase order for 352 filters may be missed if the only condition focused on is whether the inventory position is at or above the target.

The point is that inventory planners need to keep a close eye on on-hand inventory, on-order inventory and changing forecasts, not just the inventory position, to ensure that service levels are achieved and that reasonable inventory levels are maintained. Most inventory management software systems have extensive exception handling capabilities that bring to the users' attention situations that may require actions to alleviate poten-tial overstock or understock situations. It is worthwhile to check that the right exceptions are being identified in a timely manner and that supply managers are taking the right steps in response to the exceptions. Often, the exception management capability of these systems needs to be care-fully calibrated so that not too many or too few exceptions are generated.

Lead Time Variability

The target inventory position calculation in the oil filter example assumes that the replenishment lead time is 2 weeks. In practice, the actual replen-ishment lead times vary for a variety of reasons:

- A supplier may not have enough finished goods inventory to fill an order when it is received.
- A supplier may not have enough capacity to produce the order when it is received, or the supplier's production line may not be set up to produce the requested product and may not be scheduled to produce it for a protracted period.
- A supplier may not have enough raw material available to produce the order either because of an industry wide shortage or because of a temporary stock-out.
- There may be logistics congestion—for example, delays in unloading cargo at busy ports or weather related delays.
- There may be lack of available transportation capacity.

The question arises of how to modify the target inventory position to account for lead time variability. The answer is that moderate fluctuations in lead times—that is, those that cause fluctuations of around 10%–20% of the average—are best handled by simply using a planned lead time that is about 10 or 20% higher than the average. In the oil filter example, the orders are almost always received at the warehouse toward the middle of the second week after they ordered. By specifying the planned lead time as 2 weeks, you are effectively providing a reasonable protection against moderate delays. Together with an effective exception management sys-tem that highlights when orders have been delayed and allows users to respond proactively, adding a small amount to planned lead times should be sufficient to protect against moderate lead time delays.

Some textbooks argue that lead time variability should be incorporated explicitly into the calculation of the target inventory position.[5] There are two dangers in doing this. First, there is the risk that the calculation will cause safety stock double counting because the planned lead time, on which the target inventory position is based, probably already has some protection built in to it. Second, the usual analytical approach to incorporating lead time variability into the safety stock calculation rests on the highly tenuous assumption that lead times are independent and identically distributed. The result is that the formulas may wildly over- or understate the required inventory needed to protect against lead time variability. The bottom line is that these calculations are best avoided in favor of making modest explicit adjustments to the planned lead times.

The bigger challenge is dealing with much longer lead time extensions. These kinds of lead time extensions are almost always due to systemic underlying problems that are well known in advance of placing an order. Addressing these issues requires more than just modifying the target inventory position. In some cases, all that is required is a modification in the planned lead times at appropriate times of the year. For example, there are likely to be significant delays in getting cargo through the Port of Long Beach in the month of December. Planned lead times should be adjusted accordingly at that time of year if orders are transiting that port.

In other cases, modification of planned lead times won't help much. For example, in 2009–2010, a prolonged shortage of key electronic components, including power transistors, capacitors, and diodes, used in a wide variety of products caused lead times to more than double from 6 to 10 weeks to 18 to 20 weeks. Trying to protect service levels against this shortage by holding additional safety stock would have been futile. Instead, companies scrambled to find alternative supply or, in some cases, focused on products that did not require the constrained parts. Despite those efforts, the shortages caused large losses in sales. "Network-equipment vendor Telefon AB L.M. Ericsson said shortages cost the company $400 million to $550 million in sales and delayed shipments."[6] Unfortunately, these kinds of supply disruptions occur regularly. The right answer is not to try to hold enough safety stock to protect against these events, a cure that would almost surely be worse than the disease.

Rather, having a well-thought-out playbook ready to respond to these shortages is probably the best any company can do.

Closed-Loop Inventory Control

The attitude toward setting safety stock targets in much of the inventory management literature can be summed up by the memorable phrase of Ron Popeil, "Set it and forget it." Unfortunately, what works for Ronco does not work in inventory planning. The calculation of the target inventory position depends on accuracy of the unbiased forecast, estimates of the demand coefficient of variation and distribution, and lead time estimates. These estimates are often wrong, which may lead to service-level targets that are under or overachieved. In other words, what if, after all the sophisticated efforts to set inventory policy parameters have been undertaken, the service-level targets are missed? What is to be done? Do you go back to the drawing board and try again? This problem is rarely addressed in the inventory management literature. It's as though all the focus is on how to determine the optimal ordering policy based on a series of assumptions, and none of the focus is on what to do if, despite our best efforts, that policy fails.

The answer, fortunately, is relatively simple and, in fact, leads to an approach that largely obviates the need to worry too much about the initial setting of safety stock targets through formulas. The solution is to implement a mechanism to dynamically correct the inventory policy in response to achieved service and inventory levels. The basic idea is to monitor service and inventory levels over time and modify target replenishment policy parameters based on whether the service and inventory levels are within an acceptable range. This approach is similar to control charts used widely in statistical process control. By using this control chart mechanism, you don't need to worry too much about whether inventory parameters derived via formula are correct or not: The control mechanism will automatically adjust targets based on achieved service and inventory levels.

Process for Dynamic Inventory Control

Figure 4.1 illustrates the process by which this control mechanism should work. In the first step, inventory targets are set using the best data and

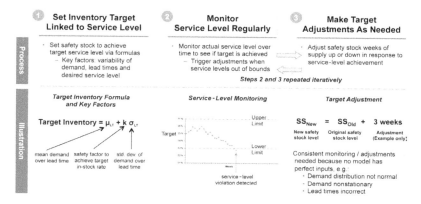

Figure 4.1. Process for dynamically adjusting inventory levels to achieve service-level targets.[7]

formulas available. In the second step, the service levels are monitored over time to see if the desired service levels are achieved. If the service levels fall within a prespecified range, no action is taken. If they fall outside this range, the inventory levels are adjusted by modifying the target inventory position. Generally this is achieved by changing the number of safety stock weeks of supply in the inventory management system. If the service levels are being underachieved, the number of weeks of supply would be increased by a specified amount—3 weeks in the example, but the actual number may vary. If the service levels are being overachieved, the weeks of supply would be reduced by a specified amount. Steps 2 and 3 are repeated on an ongoing basis to maintain the service level within the desired range. If the target service levels change during the S&OP process, these new targets can automatically drive reductions or increases in the weeks of supply to bring the service levels within the desired new range. In this way, the service-level targets are maintained over time within the target range.

One practical challenge that arises in implementing this feedback control process is monitoring service levels when the target service levels are set extremely high—for example, at 99%. The issue here is that since the highest service level that can be achieved is 100%, the process may never detect an upper-limit violation if that limit is set at 100%. And yet the inventory levels could very well be too high, and lowering the target inventory position could be achieved without negatively affecting the service levels. One way to overcome this problem is to monitor inventory levels and service levels. Then, if inventory levels go above a specified threshold even though service levels are still below the upper limit, the inventory targets could be lowered.

Case Study of Dynamic Inventory Control

While this closed-loop feedback mechanism for maintaining target service levels makes sense on an intuitive level, it is not widely utilized in industry, mostly because it is not widely known, and more important, it is not a standard capability of inventory and supply planning software systems. As a result, any company wishing to implement such a process needs to build the process and the software tools to support the process from scratch.

One example in which this feedback control mechanism was successfully deployed is a major auto parts distributor, ABC company. ABC supplies auto parts purchased from a large variety of vendors to independent retailers throughout the United States. It stores inventory in four regional distribution centers and delivers products to customers within 48 hours of order receipt using a long haul and local delivery truck fleet. ABC stocks about 100,000 SKUs at each warehouse. Many of these items are slow sellers: About 80% of these SKUs sell at a rate of less than 50 units per year. These SKUs account for about one-third of revenue, but despite their relatively low contribution to revenue, management believes that carrying this wide assortment of SKUs in all product categories is what gives the company an edge over competitors, who tend to focus on fewer, higher selling items.

Inventory planners divide the SKUs into categories A to F based on annual sales volume. For each SKU category, management has set target in-stock rates. These target rates are subject to considerable debate within the company, and several proposals for changing the way they are established have been considered. Table 4.1 shows the annual sales volume of each category, and the current target in-stock rate that management has established for each category. The target is an average over all SKUs in the category, so significant variation can exist across the SKUs in a category while still meeting the target. Of course, the ideal objective would

Table 4.1. SKU Categories and In-Stock Rate Targets

Category	Sales volume per year	In-stock rate target (%)	# of items in category
A	>500	99	3,479
B	100–500	98	18,320
C	50–100	96	19,774
D	25–50	94	30,120
E	13–25	92	45,466
F	0–12	91	145,143

be to achieve the target for each SKU in the category, but differences in demand volatility and vendor performance make that difficult to achieve in practice.

Inventory planners had set safety stock and reorder points in the purchasing system based on formulas to achieve the target in-stock rate. In the past, if the in-stock rates were not achieved, they would undertake a root cause analysis and make adjustments to the safety stock formulas to try to improve performance. This was time consuming and did not always lead to a good result. At the start of one calendar year, inventory planners agreed to a pilot in which they would apply the concept of modifying safety stock based on a dynamic feedback mechanism. The pilot focused on category D items, which consisted of approximately 30,000 SKUs.

Starting at the beginning of the calendar year, inventory planners tracked the in-stock rate of all categories of SKUs across all warehouses by week. At the start of the year, the in-stock rate for D items was close to the target in-stock rate of 94%. About a quarter of the way through the year, however, inventory planners noticed an uptick in the average out-of-stock rate. They watched in growing alarm as the out-of-stock rate continued to climb through the following 6 weeks. Further analysis revealed that among the D items, there was a set of SKUs from some underperforming vendors that appeared to be largely responsible for the increase in the out-of-stock rate. These SKUs accounted for about 35% of the SKUs in the category.

Figure 4.2 shows the out-of-stock rate by week over the calendar year for all D items (the solid), the D items from the underperforming vendors (dashed line) and the D items from all other vendors (dotted line).

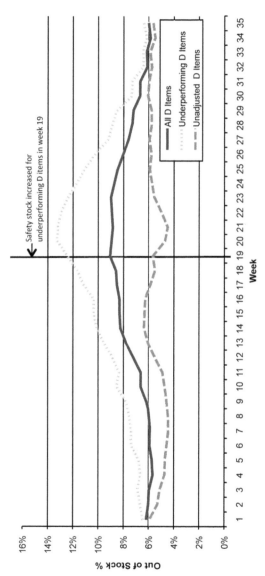

Figure 4.2. Out-of-stock rates over time for D items.

By week 19, the out-of-stock rate for all D items had climbed to 9%, and the inventory planners decided an adjustment in inventory policy was necessary to address this issue. They decided to increase the safety stock for all the SKUs from the underperforming vendors by 4 weeks. In the weeks following the increase, out-of-stock rates fell dramatically for these SKUs, and the overall target of 94% was reestablished by week 32.

This experiment convinced management that adjusting safety stock levels in response to achieved in-stock rates was an effective mechanism for ensuring that target in-stock rates were maintained over time. They proceeded to roll the process out more broadly and to implement a more robust control chart tracking mechanism that included inventory, as well as out-of-stock rates, and established well-defined control bands to determine when safety stock adjustments were to be made.

Different Service-Level Specifications

The in-stock rate measure of service level is only one of many customer-service-level metrics that companies use. Frequently, companies focus on fill rate metrics that measure the fraction of demand that is met within some time frame. For example, a typical off-the-shelf fill rate measure would report on the percent of orders that are filled from available on-hand inventory at the time the order is received from the customer. Some build-to-order manufacturers measure fill rate as the fraction of orders that are shipped within x days of order receipt. This is similar to the off-the-shelf fill rate measure but allows for some delay before orders are shipped usually based on a planned manufacturing lead time.

Complications with the fill rate metric arise when customer purchase orders comprise a large number of line items. If an order is received with, say, 100 line items and 80 of those line items can be filled on time but 20 cannot, what is the achieved service level for that order? In this situation, companies may report both an order-level fill rate and a line-item-level fill rate. The order-level fill rate in this example would be zero—that is, the order was not filled on time—but the item-level fill rate would be 80% because 80% of the line items were available to ship on time. Volume weighted, revenue weighted, and gross profit weighted line-item fill rate measures are possible as well. If orders can be split, with some line items shipped while others await fulfillment, the order-level fill rate might reflect that some fraction of the order met the service-level target while the other fraction did not.

One of the problems with focusing on fill rate service-level measures is that there is no distinction among orders that miss the service-level threshold. An order that is one day late does not affect the metric any differently than an order that is 10 days late. As a result, there is typically no management focus on those orders that are severely late as opposed to only 1 or 2 days late. And yet it is the severely late orders that are the ones that typically lead to really dissatisfied customers. So it's important not to lose sight of these outliers when tracking service-level metrics and to have appropriate management focus on these orders to keep them to a minimum.

The challenge for inventory and supply planners in this context is how to translate service-level targets of various kinds that are specified by the S&OP process into operational service-level targets that the planners can use to set inventory targets. In the case of the oil filter example, this translation is not even necessary: The service level specified by the S&OP process is an in-stock rate target at the warehouse level, and this can be used directly by the inventory planners to set inventory targets. However, in many circumstances, a translation may be necessary. For example, suppose an assemble-to-order manufacturer has set a service-level target on a set of SKUs to be 90% of orders shipped within 10 business days. If the inventory planners are responsible for setting inventory targets for the components utilized in building these SKUs to order, the challenge for them is translating the service-level target at the finished goods level into a in-stock rate target for components so that the end-customer service-level target can be met. Of course, even if the components are all available when an order drops, that is no guarantee that the order will be shipped within 10 days. Shipment depends on whether the assembly process can turn around the order within this period, which they may be able to do most of the time. However, if the assembly process cannot turn around more than 90% of orders within 10 days, even a 100% in-stock rate for components will not enable meeting the end-customer service level. In this case, some reconsideration of the service-level targets is in order.

But let's assume that the assembly process can typically turn orders around well within the 10-day window if components are available when orders drop. Then the question is what in-stock rate should inventory planners target for components in order to ensure that the service-level target will be met. In general, this is not a simple question to answer because it depends on how long replenishments take when a stock-out of a component occurs. If a stock-out of a component lasts usually only a day or two, that may be enough to allow the assembly process to still turn around the order within the 10-day window. On the other hand, if the stock-out lasts a week or longer, the orders that require the stocked out component will almost certainly be late.

How long a stock-out lasts is a complicated function of volatility of demand for the component (which may be different from the volatility of the end-product demand) and the supply replenishment process. It also depends on whether orders are backlogged. In order to determine an appropriate in-stock rate to target for components, inventory and supply planners should probably not rely on a one-size-fits-all approach. For parts that are inexpensive, a policy that effectively achieves a 100% in-stock rate by holding, say, 180 days of supply on hand may make perfect sense. For other parts, a more careful setting of the in-stock rate target may be appropriate. In these cases, a two-pronged approach is recommended:

- For initial setting of in-stock targets, utilize simulation or, if available, an analytical approximation to estimate the required in-stock targets.
- For ongoing maintenance of these targets, utilize a closed-loop inventory control mechanism to modify the inventory targets in response to achieved service levels.

Constructing a simulation or analytical model for determining the appropriate in-stock targets or inventory targets will vary in difficulty depending on the complexity of the product bills of material and the part replenishment mechanism. It will almost certainly involve a high degree of effort to collect and maintain the data necessary to utilize the model. However, the benefits of such a model go beyond just determining the in-stock rate of parts needed to meet the end-customer service-level targets. The model can be used to perform a variety of what-if analyses:

- Understanding the impact of modifying the end-customer service-level targets on inventory

- Assessing the impact of stock-outs on end-customer service levels based on different replenishment policies
- Determining how varying manufacturing lead times affects customer service levels

If you do not have this kind of model and building one is not feasible, you can always utilize a closed-loop inventory control mechanism by itself and start with an in-stock rate target based on a reasonable initial guess. That could be, for example, to target a 95% in-stock rate for all components.

Production Planning Considerations

When products need to be manufactured, a number of complicating factors arise that make a simple target inventory position policy for managing inventory impractical. The most common approach to inventory and supply planning in manufacturing environments is to use material requirements planning (MRP) logic to determine the timing of production and lot size quantities. The basic logic of MRP is well documented[8] and is embedded within the software of most Enterprise Resource Planning (ERP) systems. The general concept, originally developed by J. Orlicky, G. Plossl, O. Wight,[9] and others in the 1960s and 1970s, is to define the manufacturing process of a finished product as a set of operations with precedents, inputs, lead times, and resources required for each operation defined. The key input to the MRP system is the master production schedule (MPS), which specifies the quantity of finished products that are to be produced over time. The output of an MRP run is a plan of what operations should be performed when, what raw materials are required when, and what resources are needed when, in order to produce the finished products specified in the master production schedule.

The MRP logic in ERP systems automates much of the process of translating a sales and operations plan into a production plan. These systems generally work well and without them, keeping modern-day manufacturing plants running smoothly would be difficult if not impossible. But, like all software, MRP logic is not a panacea, and there are a number of ways in which these systems, when utilized by people who have at best only a partial understanding of how they work, can go wrong, leading to excess supply or product shortages.

Conversion of the Sales and Operations Plan to the Master Production Schedule

One key way in which things can go wrong is in translating the sales and operations plan into the MPS. In most cases, the sales and operations plan is specified at an aggregate level and the process of disaggregation to the level required for the master production schedule creates distortions. In one manufacturer of air conditioners, the S&OP process output a plan that specified required supply at a product family level. After each S&OP cycle, the plant manager, with his production planning staff, had to figure out how to take a monthly, family-level sales and operations plan and translate it into a weekly SKU-level master production schedule, which would be fed into the MRP system. This translation was performed in a spreadsheet and was based partially on the past split in sales volumes, partially on availability of certain constrained parts and partially on which SKUs the sales department was currently complaining about as likely to run out of supply. It was a seat of the pants translation process and left many customers dissatisfied and company officials frustrated as they repeatedly ended up with too much inventory of SKUs that were not in demand and too little inventory for the items that were popular.

This is a problem caused by the S&OP process not providing adequate information to production. The sales and operations plan needs to provide enough guidance to allow the plant managers to do their jobs. With too many constraints, the plant managers cannot possibly meet their objectives; with too few, they are left second guessing what the right production quantities should be. An example of too many constraints would be specifying both the aggregate number of air conditioners that should be manufactured and a service-level target. For example, manufacturing 10,000 air conditioners and providing a 98% in- stock rate. The problem is that the achievement of a 98% in-stock rate may require more or less production than 10,000 units, depending on the variability of demand. On the other hand, specifying a 98% in-stock rate for a brand provides too little guidance: Is the objective to provide 98% in-stock rate for each SKU in the brand or just an average in-stock rate of 98% across SKUs. If the latter, is it

OK to achieve 95% in-stock rate for some SKUs as long as others have in-stock rates above 98% so that the weighted average comes in close to 98%? By the same token, specifying only that 10,000 units in aggregate should be produced provides too little guidance as well because without service-level targets, the plant manager has no way to meaningfully decide how to divide this production among the SKUs that make up the brand.

Instead, the S&OP process should provide production with targets on service levels to achieve by product or product category, estimates on how much inventory should be required to meet those service levels, and demand forecast and variability data. With this information, the plant manager has the necessary guidance to create a master production schedule. He or she also has clear metrics to understand whether production was achieving service-level targets and production objectives. Too often, the plant manager objectives are tied only to overall factory throughput—for example, did the factory produce the aggregate volume of products specified by the sales and operations plan? But these objectives don't measure whether the right mix of products was produced. Plant managers' incentives can be skewed by other factors as well. For example, if absorption accounting is utilized (whereby all the costs of manufacturing, including fixed, variable, and mixed costs, are allocated to the produced units), companies will sometimes pull forward production of a product with no demand (at the expense of a product for which there is demand) in order to achieve the monthly absorption target.

It is also easy to understand in this context why it is so important for the S&OP process to take into consideration supply and capacity constraints when arriving at a realistic sales and operations plan. Without this, the sales and operations plan, even if translated to the level of detail required by the factory, will likely be unachievable. In this case, the most common response is "load and chase": Load the sales and operations plan into the MRP system, knowing full well that the plan is not achievable, and then chase the required supply and resources to build to the plan—an expensive and inefficient way to run a business.

Setting of Parameters in the ERP System

Anyone working with an ERP system to run an MRP process knows that there are a large number of parameters to set in order to get the system to work properly—for example, those governing lot sizes, lead times, and safety stock. Many of these parameters can have a material impact on manufacturing performance, and setting them correctly is important. One common problem is setting parameters that end up duplicating efforts to protect against variability that are performed elsewhere. For example, the master production schedule should already have adjustments built in to account for demand variability. But most ERP systems have capabilities to calculate safety stock to meet a target service level. If this functionality is enabled, it can end up inadvertently double counting the safety stock by adding this to the master production schedule. Ensuring that such double counting does not occur is an important responsibility of inventory and supply planners.

Another common redundancy occurs in protecting against lead time variability. Typically, the planned production lead times input into an ERP system are exaggerated to protect against modest variations in lead time. For example, if the replenishment lead time for a part is 5 days, plus or minus 2 days, the planned lead time might be entered as 7 or 8 days. This is generally fine, but if procurement personnel use the purchase advice from the ERP system as an input to decide when to place orders, they should not add additional days to the lead time to ensure that the parts arrive on time. For example, the ERP system might output a recommended purchase quantity on January 15 based on the planned lead time of 8 days. The procurement personnel might decide to place that order on January 13 because they are trying to ensure that the order arrives on time, not knowing that the MRP system has already made such an adjustment. The result is that the planned lead time is effectively 10 days, and the order will probably arrive 5 days before it needs to. This problem will not occur if the ERP system automatically generates purchase orders, which is frequently, but not always, the case.

Conversion of Requirements Output From the ERP System Into Factory Floor Inventory Policies and Replenishment Plans

Output from the MRP logic of an ERP system may not be translated into a coherent plan for shop floor execution or part procurement. For example, in a build-to-order manufacturing environment, the net requirements for component inventory is a key output from the ERP system.

It is derived from the master production schedule via a bill of material explosion, lead time offsets, and netting against on-hand (unassigned) inventory. Problems arise if procurement treats the net requirements for component inventory as an unbiased forecast and implements an inventory policy that tries to achieve a target service level by adding safety stock to the net requirements. The critical point is that the MPS is not an unbiased forecast: It already has, or is supposed to have, safety stock built in to achieve a target service level based on demand variability. By adding safety stock to a plan that already has safety stock built in, the procurement personnel are inadvertently increasing the likelihood that there will be excess inventory.

Another way in which the ERP system output may not be translated into shop floor execution is when factories use kanbans or other visual systems for controlling inventory and throughput. In these situations, the setting of kanban sizes may not be tied directly to the ERP system, and as a result, there may be little or no connection between production on the shop floor and the master production schedule.

Avoiding Redundancy in Safety Stock

A recurring problem in supply chain planning is that protection against risk and uncertainty occurs at multiple points in the planning process, resulting in redundant and excess safety stock. This sort of double counting can arise in a variety of ways, many of which I have already touched on. The following are some typical ways that redundancy can occur:

- The unbiased forecast that starts the planning process may not really be unbiased. It may already contain some buffer against demand uncertainty. This occurs most frequently when the sales force is tasked with generating an unbiased forecast. For example, sales personnel may want to protect supply, they may feel pressure to increase their forecasts to achieve some revenue target, or they simply overestimate demand because they see the world through rose-colored glasses.
- The sales and operations plan incorporates demand variability by positioning the plan to achieve a certain fraction of the demand distribution. However, inventory and supply planners

either don't know this or don't trust the process and therefore increase their inventory levels to account for demand variability on top of what the S&OP process has already done.
- Planned lead times in the ERP systems are likely already inflated but planning personnel may either not know this or not feel they are providing enough protection against lead time variability and therefore adjust safety stock targets upward.

The root cause of these problems are independent silos of functionality in an organization that are not aware of, or do not trust, the actions of other silos. Inventory and supply planners are responsible for identifying and rooting out planning redundancies like this. Different mechanisms can be deployed to mitigate and root out these redundancies:

- End-to-end accountability. If there is too much safety stock due to redundancy, the service-level targets and inventory targets will be exceeded. By the same token, if no single organization is held accountable for meeting customer-service-level targets, the service-level target can be missed and no single person or organization is held accountable. By implementing a system of end-to-end accountability, the company can ensure that these redundancies get surfaced and addressed.
- Dynamic inventory control. If redundancy exists, it can be systematically reduced or eliminated by implementing a dynamic inventory control system that automatically adjusts safety stock levels in response to achieved service levels. This mechanism also addresses the problem of service levels being underachieved.
- Ensuring that different sources of uncertainty are only protected against once in the planning process. This is easier said than done. It may involve the following:
  - Careful mapping of business processes and system functionality to understand where overlap, redundancy, and miscommunication occur
  - Incentive realignment
  - Process and system changes

Strategic Issues in Inventory and Supply Planning

The strategic issues raised in this final section could easily form the basis of a separate book. I touch on them here because they are relevant to the general question of how companies should best position themselves to meet customer demand, and they obviously have a major impact on inventory and supply planning activities.

A central strategic issue that companies need to wrestle with occasionally is deciding where and in what form it makes most sense to store inventory. The basic questions are these:

- Are you storing inventory in forms and locations that make the most sense from both a customer serviceability perspective and an inventory perspective?
- Are there ways to reconfigure your supply chain so that inventory levels can be decreased and service levels increased?

For example, for products that are assembled from components, such as computers or most consumer durables, does it make more sense to store inventory as finished goods, supplying customers from distribution centers that stock finished goods or to stock inventory as parts or semi-finished goods and then build and ship the final products based on firm orders? Or in a distribution network, does it make sense to stock the same product in different distribution centers or to stock the product in only one central location?

These questions are closely tied to the manufacturing and distribution strategy of a company and to the network structure of a supply chain. The inquiry can be extended to include not only where and in what form to store inventory but also where manufacturing sites and distribution centers should be located, where products should be sourced from, and what the distribution network should look like. These are strategic questions that need to be asked and probably more frequently than most companies appreciate. There is inertia in most supply chains, a tendency to continue to do things as they have been done even though the original reasons for doing them have long since changed.

These questions arise because of the intrinsic trade-offs among the different costs of operating a supply chain. In the manufacturing scenario, the primary benefit of stocking inventory in raw material or semifinished form is risk pooling, which occurs because parts are shared across multiple finished products and which can result in a substantial reduction in required safety stock. The costs of this strategy are typically lower asset utilization and slower ability to respond to customer orders. Lower asset utilization occurs because the option of smoothing production by building ahead of demand is curtailed in a build-to-order environment. In the distribution setting, the primary benefit of stocking inventory in a central location is again risk pooling and lower management complexity. The potential costs are increased transportation costs and longer delivery times to customers.

Companies address these trade-offs in a variety of different ways. Some aggressively pursue build-to-order manufacturing strategies, leveraging advances in manufacturing technology that have made mass customization an increasingly viable option both in terms of cost and ability to deliver custom configured products. In the textbook publishing industry, for example, printing technology breakthroughs now allow print-on-demand that enables publishing custom textbooks for specific courses in small quantities at competitive prices. Many companies pursue hybrid manufacturing models where some product is built to order and some to forecast. Automobile manufacturers typically build some cars to specific end-customer orders while others are built to a forecast and shipped to dealers who sell them. Other companies have reconfigured products to enable postponement and late-stage customization strategies, whereby products are designed to allow end-product differentiation to occur toward the end of the manufacturing process or even in distribution centers. Perhaps the most well-known case study of postponement is the Hewlett-Packard printer supply chain.[10]

These questions are central to how a company operates. Their resolution affects many company stakeholders, potentially requires significant change in the physical layout of the supply chain as well as in how demand is fulfilled and supply replenished, and has significant cost and revenue implications. As a result, the process for answering these questions should involve a broad spectrum of stakeholders, including sales, marketing, production, procurement, and logistics. The first step is identifying the right team of people who have the authority to make these decisions, can represent different perspectives fairly, and are open-minded and creative about possible solutions. They may or may not be the same people involved in the S&OP process.

These individuals will disagree about the right outcome. Providing a data-driven, analytical basis for looking at the different options is often critical to arriving at a good solution. Computer models of supply chains that capture the trade-offs between different operating strategies can serve as powerful tools to help quantify the cost and benefits of different strategies. These models never capture all dimensions of these issues, but used judiciously, they can shed light and diffuse heated emotional debates.

Many books and articles have been written about supply chain network modeling, and numerous software solutions are available to help companies formulate and solve supply chain network optimization problems. The following are some points to keep in mind as you devise an approach to solving this type of problem:

- Much of the literature and most of the software solutions in this area tend to focus on the problem of optimization— that is, how to find an optimal solution. In practice, it's far more important to be able to assess performance of different proposed scenarios than to solve an optimization problem. The first step in analyzing a supply chain network is to agree on the metrics to judge a supply chain network's effectiveness: What costs should be included at what level of detail, what service-level metrics should be utilized, and what other metrics—perhaps less easily quantified—should be considered? A useful starting exercise is to layout two or three candidate solutions and construct a model for assessing the performance of each of them. Often, this performance evaluation model is sufficient to guide an organization to a solution, without resorting to optimization. Even if an optimization model is called for, the performance evaluation model should serve as the basis for the optimization model.
- Developing a supply chain network model, like any other modeling exercise, always requires a trade-off between fidelity and usability. Beginners and those not versed in model building tend to fall into the trap of "more is better"—more detail, more complexity, more inputs, and more outputs equal more

credibility—and develop models that collapse under their own weight. I have seen far too many supply chain network models relegated to the dustbin because the effort to maintain and utilize the model was too great. Transparency of a model is key to getting acceptance, and the more complex a model is, the less transparent it tends to be.

- Data collection and analysis is a significant part of the effort of building any supply chain network model. Construction or configuration of a software model is not usually the bottleneck. Make sure data collection gets under way early and be specific about the level of detail and scope of data needed. Significant effort is almost always required to analyze and transform the data that is collected (usually in transactional format) into a form that is suitable for use in the model.

- Consider developing multiple models. It is not the case that all strategic questions about a supply chain network should necessarily be answered with the same model. It is often easier to create separate models to answer different questions. For example, it may make sense to create a deterministic model for assessing network structure and a separate stochastic model for figuring out stocking location and product postponement strategy.

- When it comes to constructing the supply chain model itself, you have the usual make-or-buy decision. You can use off-the-shelf software packages,[11] or you can also build your own model using generic software modeling tools.[12] Building your own model provides a level of modeling flexibility that packaged software solutions can't provide. It also has the advantage that you can build the model incrementally, adding complexity one layer at a time until a model of sufficient usefulness is obtained. Of course, every situation is different, and the right choice will depend on trade-offs between total cost of ownership, development time, and functionality.

- Don't forget about big cost drivers that are easy to overlook but can have a major impact on the decision, such as country, state, and local tax incentives.

Case Study: A Packaged Food Company

Acme company, a major U.S. producer of packaged food, manufactures products at several facilities in the United States and distributes these products to customers (largely retail chains) via regional distribution centers. Acme, like many companies in the packaged food industry, offers the same product in a variety of different packaging options, including some that are used only for specific customers. A given product may have as many as 20 different ways in which it is packaged. In the current way that Acme operates its supply chain, all varieties of packaging are built to a forecast at factories and shipped to distribution centers in advance of firm customer orders. When customer orders are received, they are filled from available finished goods inventory out of the nearest distribution center. If inventory is not available in the right packaging, one of three things can happen: (a) the customer is forced to wait until a replenishment is received from the factory, (b) the order may be filled out of another distribution center (at additional transportation cost to Acme), or (c) inventory at the distribution center that is of the right product but wrong package type is repackaged and used to fill the order (also at additional expense to Acme).

Because a large quantity of demand for Acme products is seasonal, and because the factories produce in large batches with significant setup times between production runs, the product is manufactured and packaged well in advance of customer orders. Since there is no significant storage space for finished goods inventory at the factories, the finished product is immediately shipped to distribution centers based on forecasted demand. Because these forecasts are not reliable, this build-and-ship-to-forecast process is causing mismatches in supply and demand, with significant negative impact on customer service levels, transshipment costs, repackaging costs, and excess and obsolete inventory costs.

One possible solution to address these problems is to implement a packaging postponement strategy whereby final packaging of finished goods would be done at distribution centers mostly at the time that customer orders were received. In this scenario, finished goods in a generic, unpackaged form would be shipped from the factory and stored at the distribution centers. When customer orders are received, the requested products would be packaged per the order using packaging equipment at the distribution centers and then shipped to the customer. The big perceived benefit of such a change would be risk pooling: The generic finished product inventory could be used to satisfy a large variety of customer orders, resulting in lower safety stock, lower or eliminated costs due to transshipment, repackaging, excess and obsolete inventory, and improved customer service.

At the same time, Acme's products continue to grow in popularity, and projected sales growth over the next 5 years indicates a need for additional manufacturing capacity. Much debate in the company has been generated about where this additional capacity should be added and when it is really needed. Some people believe that additional capacity should be added to existing manufacturing facilities while others argue that a new site is required. Some feel that the additional capacity is not needed for many years while others believe a capacity crunch will be felt much earlier. Finally, some people think that the new manufacturing module should be smaller but more flexible—that is, able to produce a wider variety of products with smaller setups—while others believe that a larger capacity module with less flexibility will be more cost effective.

The supply chain group at Acme was tasked with finding solutions to both the postponement and manufacturing capacity problems. To help assess the impact of various solutions, the team decided to build a supply chain model that would enable assessing the cost and service-level impact of different solutions. At first, the team believed that one model capable of addressing the capacity and postponement questions at the same time was perhaps the best approach. But after some consideration, it was decided that the two issues, while related, were largely independent and could be treated separately: The company could pursue a postponement strategy regardless of whether and where manufacturing capacity was increased.

As a result, two models were developed, one to help assess the costs of different manufacturing capacity expansion options and another to assess the value of a packaging postponement strategy. The manufacturing capacity model was a fairly standard network optimization model formulated as a mixed integer program. The postponement model was a stochastic model built to assess the impact of the postponement strategy on service levels and inventory levels. It was realized in the form of a Monte Carlo simulation. Both models were developed from scratch using software components to construct the solution. The front ends of both solutions were built in Excel with the actual modeling done using a combination of Visual Basic for Applications (VBA) and optimization libraries.

Both models provided valuable insight to the team and helped to drive to a consensus. For the manufacturing capacity issue, the model demonstrated that the supply chain cost differential between the different options being considered was not highly significant. As a result, other considerations became more prominent. For example, a major consideration turned out to be the value of tax abatement incentives offered by states and municipalities. And qualitative issues like the perceived business friendliness of states and the risks associated with severe weather became more important. But the network model was instrumental in convincing the team that the cost differential was not the deciding factor. Also, the model was helpful in deciding when the additional capacity was needed. The supply chain team has now begun the process of drawing up engineering and architectural plans for the new site.

The postponement model helped to convince the team that the postponement strategy will help to reduce finished goods inventory and improve service levels. The model demonstrated that under a wide variety of different scenarios and assumptions, the benefits of postponement clearly outweigh the costs of deploying the strategy, including the additional packaging equipment at the distribution centers. The supply chain team is now in the process of carrying out a pilot to prove the effectiveness of the postponement strategy and work out implementation issues. They expect to roll the process out across the company within the next few years.

Afterword

"Our company is different." That is the common refrain I have heard from individuals at many companies, usually as a preface to saying why the challenges they are facing are particularly difficult or why standard solutions don't apply to their businesses. Yet, while the statement is true, it does not follow that the challenges companies face are fundamentally different. In fact, the similarities are often striking even in markedly different industries. That is the premise underlying the themes addressed in this book: that the challenges of supply chain planning are remarkably similar across different companies and different industries. And while the challenges are the same, the solutions do not necessarily have to be identical, just as there are many architectural solutions to the problem of building a bridge.

The simple framework for thinking about supply chain planning presented in this book—one that consists of the three separate but interrelated processes of demand planning, sales and operations planning, and inventory and supply planning—is applicable to all businesses, even those not in manufacturing or distribution. The same can be said of the analytical approaches to solving many of the supply chain planning problems presented here.

In keeping this book brief, I have excluded or abbreviated many relevant topics. There is ample room for expanding on solution approaches, many of which are described only briefly or not at all, as well as for providing additional case studies that shed light on how these solutions can be successfully deployed. But for those who are trying to solve supply chain planning problems, the ideas presented here should provide a good starting point for tackling them.

Notes

Foreword

1. Brynjolfsson et al. (2011).

Chapter 1

1. Gladwell (2001), pp.78–79.
2. Bureau of Economic Analysis (2010).
3. Singh (1968), p. 8.
4. Fisher (1997), p. 111.
5. See, for example, Taleb (2004, 2007) and Mlodinow (2008).

Chapter 2

1. Foster (1924), p. vi.
2. Wallace (1928), pp. 3–4.
3. For a detailed review of statistical forecasting methods, see, for example, Makridakis et al. (1998). For a textbook introduction to statistical forecasting, see, for example, Nahmias (2008).
4. Past sales are only a surrogate for past demand, though a fairly reliable one in most cases. The two most frequent situations in which past sales need to be adjusted to obtain improved estimates of demand are when stock-outs occur and when large numbers of returns occur. More about these two situations later.
5. For the cynical, to the extent that forecasting using past sales is like looking in the rear view mirror to see what is coming down the road, at the very least one should make sure the rear view mirror is clean.
6. There may also be a lull in sales in prior weeks if the promotion is advertised in advance.
7. Examples of some full-featured demand planning software systems: Demantra (Oracle Corp.), i2 Demand Manager (JDA Software Group, Inc.), JDA Demand (JDA Software Group, Inc.), Advanced Planner and Optimizer (SAP Inc.), Logility Demand Optimization (American Software, Inc.), and Demand Management (TXT e-solutions S.p.A.). In addition, there are a number of software solutions that provide statistical forecasting capabilities, for example,

Forecast Pro (Business Forecast Systems, Inc.), Autobox (Automatic Forecasting Systems, Inc.), SAS Forecast Server (SAS), SPSS Forecasting (IBM Corp.), PSI Planner for Windows (Logistics Planning Associates, LLC), SYSTAT 13 (Systat Software, Inc.), and STATGRAPHICS (StatPoint Technologies, Inc.).

8. The M3–IJF Competition held in 1997 is one example.

9. In fact, one of the reasons that the Holt-Winters and exponential smoothing approaches were developed was to reduce the storage requirements for generating and updating forecasts over time.

10. Demand for replacement parts might follow a compound Poisson process if the failure rate of the part is assumed to follow an exponential distribution.

11. This would obviously depend on the logic in the purchasing system. Most systems will have logic to round quantities to integers when purchase quantities need to be integer values. The rounding logic can be quite intricate and 0.75 units may get rounded to one, zero, or possibly a higher number.

12. Perhaps the most publicized example of mitigating reliance on a forecast through a quick response initiative is Sport Obermeyer, as described in Fisher (1997) and Hammond and Raman (1996).

13. See, for example, Makridakis and Hibon (2000).

14. The mMAPE metric is one that I have come across in practice, but I have not been able to find a reference to it in any textbook or journal.

15. This is another reason not to use sales net of returns in forecasting.

16. Logility Voyager Solutions (2011).

Chapter 3

1. Ling and Goddard (1988), pp. 4–5.

2. See, for example, Dougherty and Gray (2006); Wallace (2004); and Sheldon (2006).

3. See, for example, Nahmias (2008), ch. 5, and Silver and Peterson (1985), ch. 10.

4. In fact, very few mathematical extensions to the newsvendor problem have been published precisely because it is so difficult to extend the model to include additional factors.

5. See, for example, Nahmias (2008), p. 242.

6. This source wishes to remain anonymous.

7. The planned revenue, which is the planned production quantity times the price summed over all products, is different from the expected revenue.

8. Examples include JDA software, Oracle, SAP APO, Logility, and so on.

9. Examples include AIMMS (Paragon Decision Technology Inc.), AMPL (AMPL Optimization LLC), GAMS (GAMS Development Corporation), IBM ILOG OPL Development Studio (IBM), MPL Modeling System (Maximal Software, Inc.), Risk Solver Platform (Frontline Systems Inc.), LINGO (LINDO

Systems, Inc.), and SAS (SAS Institute Inc.). For a review of optimization modeling environments, see Yurkiewicz (2010).

10. Ling and Goddard (1988), p. 5.

11. Examples include tools that are add-ins to Excel, such as @Risk, Risk Solver Platform, and Crystal Ball, as well as more heavy duty statistical analysis packages, such as SAS, Matlab, Mathematica, R, Minitab, and SPSS.

12. Examples of S&OP software vendors include Cognos (IBM), Steelwedge, Logility, SAP, and JDA.

Chapter 4

1. Examples of operations management texts are Heizer and Render (1996); Russell and Taylor (1995); Chase and Aquilano (1995); and McClain et al. (1992). Examples of advanced operations modeling text are Graves et al. (1993); Tersine (1994); and Silver and Peterson (1985).

2. Since anything you order today will not arrive for another 10 days, if you are short of inventory to meet demand over the next 10 days, the order you place today will not help alleviate this problem unless orders are backlogged.

3. $N^{-1}(x)$ is the inverse of the cumulative distribution of a standard normal random variable.

4. FOB stands for "free on board" and refers to the point at which the product becomes the responsibility of the buyer.

5. See, for example, Nahmias (2008), pp. 266–267.

6. Mattioli (2010).

7. This chart was created in collaboration with the Boston Consulting Group.

8. See, for example, Heizer and Render (1996).

9. See, for example, Plossl (1975) and Orlicky et al. (1972).

10. Kopczak and Lee (2001).

11. Examples of software packages for supply chain network analysis and optimization include IBM ILOG Supply Chain Optimization, i2 Supply Chain Strategist (owned by JDA Software), and SAP SCM.

12. Examples of software for building network optimization solutions from scratch include AMPL, Risk Solver Platform, and SAS.

References

Brynjolfsson, E., Hitt, L. M., & Kim, H. H. (2011, April). Strength in numbers: How does data-driven decisionmaking affect firm performance? *Social Science Research Network*. Retrieved June 23, 2011, from http://ssrn.com/abstract=1819486

Bureau of Economic Analysis. (2010, October). Real inventories, sales, and inventory-sales ratios for manufacturing and trade, 2006:IV–2010:II. Bureau of Economic Analysis. Retrieved June 22, 2011, from http://www.bea.gov/scb/pdf/2010/10%20October/1010_ISR.pdf

Chase, R. B., & Aquilano, N. J. (1995). *Production and operations management*. Chicago, IL: Richard D. Irwin.

Dougherty, J., & Gray, C. (2006). *Sales & operations planning-best practices: Lessons learned*. Belmont, NH: Partners for Excellence.

Fisher, M. L. (1997, March–April). What is the right supply chain for your product? *Harvard Business Review*, 105–116.

Foster, W. T. (1924). Introduction. In W. M. Persons (Ed.), *The problem of business forecasting: Papers presented at the eighty-fifth annual meeting of the American statistical association, Washington, D.C., December 27–29, 1923*. Boston, MA: Houghton Mifflin.

Gladwell, M. (2001, November 26). Smaller: The disposable diaper and the meaning of progress. *The New Yorker*, 74–79.

Graves, S. C., Rinnooy Kan, A. H. G., & Zipkin, P. H. (Eds.). (1993). *Logistics of production and inventory*. Amsterdam, the Netherlands: North- Holland.

Hammond, J. H., & Raman, A. (1996). *Sport Obermeyer, Ltd.* (Report Number 9–695–022). Boston, MA: Harvard Business Publishing.

Heizer, J., & Render, B. (1996). *Production and operations management*. Englewood Cliffs, NJ: Prentice-Hall.

Kopczak, L. R., & Lee, H. (2001). *Hewlett-Packard Co.: DeskJet printer supply chain (A) and (B)* (Report Number GS3A–PDF–ENG and GS3B–PDF– ENG). Boston, MA: Harvard Business Publishing.

Ling, R. C., & Goddard, W. E. (1988). *Orchestrating success: Improve control of the business with sales & operations planning*. Hoboken, NJ: John Wiley & Sons.

Logility Voyager Solutions. (2011). Voyager demand planning: Raise forecast accuracy with powerful demand planning software. Retrieved June 22, 2011, from http://www.logility.com/solutions/demandoptimization/voyager-demand -planning

Makridakis, S., & Hibon, M. (2000). The M3-Competition: Results, conclusions and implications. *International Journal of Forecasting 16*, 451–476.

Makridakis, S. G., Wheelwright, S. C., & Hyndman, R. J. (1998). *Forecasting: Methods and applications* (3rd ed.). New York, NY: John Wiley & Sons.

Mattioli, D. (2010, August 5). From snowmobiles to cellphones, a scramble for parts. *The Wall Street Journal*. Retrieved June 22, 2011, from http://online .wsj.com/article/SB10001424052748704905004575405491505513242 .html#articleTabs%3Darticle

McClain, J. O., Thomas, L. J., & Mazzola, J. B. (1992). *Operations management.* Englewood Cliffs, NJ: Prentice-Hall.

Mlodinow, L. (2008). *The drunkard's walk: How randomness rules our lives.* New York, NY: Random House.

Nahmias, S. (2008). *Production and operations analysis* (6th ed.). Columbus, OH: McGraw-Hill/Irwin.

Orlicky, J. A., Plossl, G. W., & Wight, O. W. (1972). Structuring the bill of material for MRP. *Production & Inventory Management (Journal of APICS)*, 4th Q.

Plossl, G. (1975). *Orlicky's material requirements planning.* Columbus, OH: McGraw-Hill.

Russell, R. S., & Taylor, B. W. (1995). *Production and operations management.* Englewood Cliffs, NJ: Prentice-Hall.

Sheldon, D. H. (2006). *World class sales & operations planning.* Fort Lauderdale, FL: J. Ross Publishing.

Silver, E. A., & Peterson, R. (1985). *Decision systems for inventory management and production planning.* New York, NY: John Wiley & Sons.

Singh, J. (1968). *Great ideas of operations research.* New York, NY: Dover Publications.

Taleb, N. N. (2004). *Fooled by randomness: The hidden role of chance in life and in the markets.* New York, NY: Random House.

Taleb, N. N. (2007). *The black swan: The impact of the highly improbable.* New York, NY: Random House.

Tersine, R. J. (1994). *Principles of inventory and materials management.* Englewood Cliffs, NJ: Prentice-Hall.

Wallace, T. F. (2004). *Sales & operations planning: The how-to handbook.* Cincinnati, OH: T. F. Wallace & Company.

Wallace, W. (1928). *Business forecasting and its practical application* (2nd ed.). London, UK: Sir Isaac Pitman & Sons.

Yurkiewicz, J. (2010). Forecasting: What can you predict for me? *OR/MS Today 37*(3), 36–39.

Index

The letter *f* following a page number denotes a figure

Announcing the Business Expert Press Digital Library

Concise E-books Business Students Need for Classroom and Research

This book can also be purchased in an e-book collection by your library as

- a one-time purchase,
- that is owned forever,
- allows for simultaneous readers,
- has no restrictions on printing,
- can be downloaded as PDFs from within the library community.

Our digital library collections are a great solution to beat the rising cost of textbooks. E-books can be loaded into their course management systems or onto students' e-book readers.

The **Business Expert Press** digital libraries are very affordable, with no obligation to buy in future years.

For more information, please visit **www.businessexpertpress.com/librarians**. To set up a trial in the United States, please contact **Sheri Allen** at *sheri.allen@globalepress.com*; for all other regions, contact **Nicole Lee** at *nicole.lee@igroupnet.com*.

OTHER TITLES IN OUR
SUPPLY AND OPERATIONS MANAGEMENT COLLECTION
Collection Editor: **Steven Nahmias**

A Primer on Negotiating Corporate Purchase Contracts by Patrick Penfield

Production Line Efficiency: A Comprehensive Guide for Managers
   by Sabry Shaaban and Sarah Hudson

Orchestrating Supply Chain Opportunities: Achieving Stretch Goals Efficiently
   by Ananth Iyer and Alex Zelikovsky

Transforming US Army Supply Chains: Strategies for Management Innovation
   by Greg H. Parlier

Design, Analysis, and Optimization of Supply Chains: A System Dynamics Approach
   by William Killingsowth